Preaching Through the Bible

Genesis 24–50

Michael Eaton

Sovereign World

Sovereign World
PO Box 777
Tonbridge
Kent, TN11 0ZS
England

By the same author:
Ecclesiastes (Tyndale Commentary) – IVP
Living a Godly Life – Paternoster
Enjoying God's Worldwide Church – Paternoster
Living Under Grace (Romans 6–7) – Paternoster
A Theology of Encouragement – Paternoster
1 Samuel (Preaching through the Bible) – Sovereign World
2 Samuel (Preaching through the Bible) – Sovereign World
1, 2, 3 John (Focus on the Bible) – Christian Focus
Hosea (Focus on the Bible) – Christian Focus
1–2 Thessalonians (Preaching Through the Bible) – Sovereign World
Genesis 1–11 (Preaching Through the Bible) – Sovereign World
Mark (Preaching Through the Bible) – Sovereign World

ISBN: 1-85240-269 5

Typeset by CRB Associates, Reepham, Norfolk
Printed and bound in Great Britain by
Cox & Wyman Ltd, Reading, Berkshire

Preface

There is need of a series of biblical expositions which are especially appropriate for English-speaking people throughout the world. Such expositions need to be laid out in such a way that they will be useful to those who like to have their material or (if they are preachers) to put across their material in clear points. They need to avoid difficult vocabulary and advanced grammatical structures. They need to avoid European or North American illustrations. *Preaching Through the Bible* seeks to meet such a need. Although intended for an international audience I have no doubt that their simplicity will be of interest to many first-language speakers of English as well.

These expositions are based upon the Hebrew and Greek texts. The New American Standard Version and the New International Version of the Bible are recommended to the reader but at times the expositor will simply translate the Hebrew or Greek himself.

It is not our purpose to deal with minute exegetical detail, although the commentator has to do work of this nature as part of his preliminary preparation. But just as a housewife likes to serve a good meal rather than display her pots and pans, so we are concerned with the 'good meal' of Scripture, rather than the 'pots and pans' of dictionaries, disputed interpretations and the like. Only occasionally will such matters have to be discussed. Similarly matters of 'Introduction' do not receive detailed discussion, but only as much as is necessary for the exposition to be clear. On occasions a simple outline of some 'introductory' matters will be included, perhaps in an appendix, but generally the first chapter of this book gets straight into the exposition.

Although on the surface written simply these expositions aim at a high level of scholarship, and attempt to put the theological and practical message of each book of the Bible in a clear and down-to-earth manner. Simplicity of style is not simplicity of content. God's word needs to be expounded with thoroughness but the language needs to remain easy and accessible. Some progress in this direction is attempted in these expositions.

Michael A. Eaton

Contents

Contents

Author's Preface

This third book on Genesis, like two previous ones, has arisen from my experience of preaching through this part of the Bible. Some years ago I gave expositions of the whole of Genesis on Trans-World Radio. Then in 1994 I preached in Nairobi on the life of Joseph. Recently I have been preaching parts of Genesis 24–50 again when preaching in various parts of southern Africa. These chapters are the side-effects of these various attempts at preaching through Genesis. I was grateful to churches and friends in Johannesburg, Pietmaritzburg, Mtubatuba and Durban who were receptive to much of this material during 1996.

I am grateful, as always, to Chris Mungeam for his enthusiasm and zeal for God's work, to Jenny, to Tina Gysling, my daughter, who works through my material, to my son Calvin who, when computers gnash their teeth, rescues my soul from their destructions, and whose comments on my expositions often get added to these pages.

Michael A. Eaton

Chapter 1

The Guidance of God
(Genesis 24:1–12)

The book of Genesis is the most basic of all of the books of
the Bible. It gives us the essentials of what we need to know
about God and salvation, covering considerable areas of the
teaching that Christians need. If we were only able to have
one book of the Bible, I think it would have to be Genesis! It
has in it what we need to know about creation and sin and
judgement. It has the promise of a Saviour. It has the model
of faith, Abraham. In principle it covers all of the highlights
of the Christian faith.

Genesis 1:1–11:26 gives us the background and setting to
the plan of salvation. It tells us why there is need of a
Saviour.

Genesis 11:27–25:18 tells us the story of Terah, Abraham
and Ishmael. In Abraham it gives us a model – although
imperfect – believer. Christians are the 'children of Abraham'.
Abraham is God's example of what it means to believe in the
promise of God.

At the point where we pick up the story we are at the end
of the life of Abraham and he is just about to pass the
leadership of the household of faith to Isaac. The story will
show us again how the famous heroes of Israel were men of
faith and despite great personal weaknesses inherited the
promises of God. But first we see how Abraham prepared
the way for his son.

Isaac needed a wife, but Canaanite women did not make
good wives! It was a time when Abraham needed the very
special guidance and help of God.

Many people have difficulties over the matter of guidance. 'If only I knew God's will,' they say.

Guidance is God's work more than it is ours. God will guide if we are in tune with Him. A lot of the time we do not need special guidance. It is clear when we read the stories of the great men and women of faith in the Bible that they did not have special guidance all the time.

We should not think of guidance as being like following a diagram or a builder's construction-plans. If one bit of the building goes wrong there is disaster. But God's guidance is more like following a map as you walk along or drive along in a car, in an area you only half-know. From time to time you look at the map. Occasionally you get lost and then you look at the map again to find your way back to where you should be. It is something that you are doing as you go along. Genesis 24 is not a perfect account of how to find a wife! There are things in it that are cultural and were unique to the days in which Abraham lived. I can mention four of them.

1. You don't have to marry a wife without seeing her, as Isaac did.

2. Your father does not have to arrange your wife for you. This is done in some cultures, especially in India, but it is not a law for all time and for all societies.

3. You do not have to send a servant to find a wife for your son.

4. You do not have to marry someone in your own tribe, as Abraham found one of his own people for Isaac.

Following the Bible's teaching is not the same as imitating the culture of Bible times. Parts of this story are Mesopotamian culture and can be left aside.

1. **The situation was a time of special need and so Abraham could expect God's guidance**. He was old (24:1). There was a danger that Isaac might want to marry a Canaanite, and Abraham made his servant swear that this would never happen (24:2–3). Abraham felt his son should marry someone from his own people in Haran (24:4). It was not that he was being racist. It was not that he was being narrow-minded

about Isaac's marrying someone from his own tribe. The point was more a spiritual one. He wanted Isaac to marry someone who shared his faith and there were people who shared his faith back in his home area.

It is important to marry someone from the people of God. Whether they have the same nationality or tribe is not so important. What is important is that the person concerned should be saved and that you flow with them spiritually. Abraham is deeply committed to the principle that on no account should Isaac marry an unspiritual and unconverted Canaanite. It is this that he feels about so strongly.

2. **He is very concerned that the next generation should move forward not backwards spiritually**. The servant raises a problem. Maybe there will not be any woman willing to come with him. Should Isaac go back to his father's homeland and persuade a girl to come with him (24:5)? Abraham's answer is 'no'. On no account must Isaac go back to Haran. It would be going against everything God had told Abraham. God had sworn an oath that the future of Abraham's family would be in Canaan (24:6–7). (This can be said now since the event of Genesis 22:16–17 has taken place. If this story were before Genesis 22:16–17 Abraham could not be saying what he is saying.) He is sure that the servant will find the right person. But if God does not do things this way He will send help in another way. Certainly Isaac must not go back on the guidance that has already been given.

There are some spiritual principles here. One is that a believer is not always a hundred per cent certain of the will of God. We do not have to feel guilty if at any point we are not absolutely sure about God's will.

Another principle is this. Faith often takes the form of instinct. One often has the feeling that a certain thing is the right way to go but you are not 100% certain.

Another principle is that there are certain principles one should never go back on. Abraham is certain that Isaac must never marry a pagan. And he is certain that Isaac should not go back on the way the family have been led by God until this point (24:8). *'Do not take my son back there,'* he says firmly.

So the servant takes the oath (24:9), gets ready (24:10), and leaves for Aram Naharaim. Eventually he arrives at the Aramean town of Nahor. He stops to make the camels drink water (24:11).

At this point, **he is concerned to make his task a matter of prayer**. He has arrived in the area where he has to look for a wife for Isaac, and he is not sure where to start. So he prays, *'Give me success today'* (24:12). It is quite a bold prayer. He is praying that he might have the answer 'Today!' I am sure many young men looking for a wife would like to pray that prayer. 'Give the answer today!' But God does not always guarantee to be quite so speedy! The servant did not have much time. He could not stay in Nahor for many weeks. He needed God's answer speedily and he felt led to pray in the way he did. You will not always be able to pray, 'Give the answer today!' The principle is: pray in the way you feel led to pray. But you must pray.

Chapter 2

Seeking God's Guidance
(Genesis 24:13–67)

It is permissible to ask for an indication of God's will in the events that happen. Abraham's servant asks God to give him a sign (24:13–14). There are occasions when we are led by the Holy Spirit to ask for something that will give us a signal that we are in the will of God and that God is blessing us. It brings great responsibility if God does give some kind of 'sign' in answer to our prayers.

The sign is a very sensible one. The servant does not have much time. He is looking for someone who is kind and sweet and will be courteous and hospitable. He goes to the place where the unmarried girls go early in the morning to collect water. He prays that when he asks one of them for a drink, she will take her jar down from where she carries it on her head (which was the way it was done, as it is today in many parts of the world) and will give him a drink while at the same time volunteering to give water to all ten of his camels. It is a bold prayer. A woman who will do such a thing will be kindly, willing to suffer inconvenience, physically strong. hospitable and an ideal wife for Isaac.

When we have found God's will everything will fit together. The servant's prayer was dramatically answered, even before he had finished praying. A girl arrived. Everything about her was right. She was beautiful (24:16); Isaac would be pleased about that. She was unmarried and yet ready for marriage. Without knowing it she did the very things that the servant had asked God to give him as an indication of God's will

13

(24:17–19). She took trouble using great energy to draw from the well enough water to quench the thirst of ten camels (24:20). It was a time-consuming business. The servant stood by watching quietly (24:21). Then he discovered that she came from the same clan of families that had originally come from Ur and she would therefore know something of Abraham and Isaac's ideals and faith (24:22–24). She would be an ideal wife for Isaac. When God is at work everything fits. He works at both ends of a situation. He was working in the area of Nahor; He had been at work in Canaan. Now He brings the two people together in an amazing way. From far off Aramaic-speaking Haran He brought Rebecca to a husband she had never seen in Canaan. God can do it still. As a wall-placard has it:

> Two shall be born, the whole wide world apart,
> and speak different tongues, and take no thought,
> each of the other's being, and no heed.
> And these over unknown seas to unknown lands, shall
>   cross,
> escaping wrecks, defying death,
> and all unconsciously shape every act,
> and bend each wandering step unto this end.
> That one day out of darkness, they shall meet
> and read life's meaning in each other's eyes.

The family are a hospitable people and without consulting her father Rebekah offers hospitality to the servant of Abraham (24:25). At that point the man knows his prayer has been answered. He worships God in gratitude for having led him so speedily and precisely (24:26–27).

As we seek God's will there should be a holy caution. The servant had been acting cautiously. As Rebekah had been drawing the water for him at the well he had stood there quietly wondering if this really was the leading of God. We are not to ask impulsively and impatiently. The servant was no doubt in a hurry to get back but he had been careful in seeking God's will. Now he is sure he has God's answer.

After God's will has been found there will be confirmations. From this point on everything confirms that the servant has found the ideal person for Isaac and that God has truly been leading him.

God will use the false motives of others to bring about His will for us. Rebekah has a brother (24:28–29). He is a crafty and greedy man, as the rest of the story of Genesis makes clear. He is not as sweet and pleasant as Rebekah, but he sees the signs that Abraham's family is a wealthy one. When he sees the valuable gold rings and bracelets that Rebekah is wearing he says 'Come in, blessed of the LORD!' and speedily welcomes him (24:30–32).

Soon the man is telling the whole story (24:33–47) and his conviction that it has been God who has guided him in the right way (24:48). He puts his request to Laban the head of the home (24:49). It seems obviously to be God's will and they spend the night celebrating (24:50–54). Soon the servant wants to travel back to Canaan (24:55). Laban wants to delay them. He is interested in the gold! Later on in the story we shall find him delaying Jacob the future son of Rebekah, again for reasons of covetousness. But Laban's covetousness is used by God.

Soon the servant and Rebekah depart (24:56–62). When they arrived in Canaan they soon meet Isaac and it seems to be a case of love at first sight (24:63–67).

Guidance is God's work as well as our work. The servant rightly recognised God's lovingkindness and faithfulness in what had happened (24:27). It will be the same for us. God is faithful. He will guide. Sometimes He leads us even without our knowing it. He is faithful and true to us. If we belong to God through Jesus, God will be trustworthy to us and we shall look back over our lives and say 'The Lord led me.'

And yet there is a part for us to play also. Abraham and his servant showed concern for God's will. They were sensible, sensitive, prayerful. The servant showed loyalty, patience and steady trusting devotion to God. When we are the same God will guide us.

Chapter 3

Responding to God

(Genesis 24:33–67)

The story of Abraham's servant looking for a wife for Isaac is not only a classic model of guidance, but it is also a perfect illustration of what it means to respond to the leading of God. For the events that led the servant to Rebekah also brought a great challenge to Rebekah. She was receiving the guidance of God too. There came a point where Laban turned to her and said *'Will you go with this man?'* She replied *'I will'* (24:58). This is typical not only of countless marriages; it is also typical of the life of the Christian. Indeed marriage is the greatest illustration of the love between Jesus and His Church. The Christian life is a matter of putting ourselves in the hands of Jesus. The Holy Spirit comes to us and says 'Will you go with this Jesus? Will you go to Him? Will you spend the rest of your life in fellowship with Him?' And we respond and say 'I will.'

Consider the invitation

1. **She is being invited to believe that Isaac is real**. She has never actually seen Isaac but she must take it on trust that Isaac is real and that he is looking for a bride. This is the way it is when God invites us to Jesus Christ. We are told about Jesus in some way or another, and the Holy Spirit invites us to believe that Jesus is real.

2. **She is being invited to believe that all of the promises of God are attached to this man Isaac**. If she had heard anything about Isaac it surely must have included the fact that God had said to Abraham *'Through Isaac a seed shall be called to*

16

you.' The promise of worldwide blessing was attached to this son of Abraham.

It is the same with the Christian. The Christian is a person who has been invited to believe that all of the promises of God are tied up with His Son, our Lord Jesus Christ. Out of His fullness we receive every blessing that God has for us. In Him are all the treasures of wisdom and of knowledge. The purpose of God is wrapped up with the person of our Lord Jesus Christ. Outside of Him there is no salvation, no knowledge of God, no heaven, no forgiveness of sin, no heavenly inheritance. It is all attached to this person, our Lord Jesus.

She has to respond. And we have to respond. There is no experience of God's salvation for us unless we attach ourselves by faith to Jesus. He is the heir of God. He rules God's kingdom. He must reign until He has put all enemies beneath His feet. We are co-heirs with Him. When we have Him we share everything He has. We share His sonship and become children of God. We share His righteousness and become clothed with a righteousness that is not ours but is bestowed upon us with Jesus. She must not only believe the promises; she must believe that the promises of God are for her personally.

3. **She has to face the fact that responding to God's guidance will involve abandoning her old life**. She has grown up in Haran but if she responds to this invitation her old life is finished.

The Christian is a person who has made a break with the old life of sin. He has said farewell to it for ever and is committed to the new life of inheriting the promises of God.

4. **She is invited to launch out on this new life simply on the basis of the word that has come to her through Abraham's servant**. She had to believe 'the word'. It was not great endeavours or great promises that were involved. It was faith in a word that came to her. 'There is this man Isaac,' said the servant. 'All the promises of God are tied up in him. Will you go with this man?' It was not a matter of seeing; it was a matter of trusting. If she did not trust the word that

was coming to her she would never see Isaac or have any experience of the purpose of God.

Consider the urgency of the invitation

1. **The call is an urgent matter**. The servant of Abraham is in a hurry. *'I will not eat until I have told my errand,'* he says (24:33). He tells his story (24:34–48) and then he wants an answer. *'If you are going to deal kindly and truly with my master, tell me'* (24:49).

2. **The call is immediate**. The family is inclined to accept the offer. *'This thing is from the LORD,'* says Laban (24:50). All seems well for the servant and his mission. He brings out his gifts which are part of the offer (24:53) and they celebrate with great joy. However, many seem to receive the word with great joy only in theory but then they delay ever acting upon what they have heard. *'Let the girl stay with us a few days'* (24:55). But we know about Laban's delaying tactics. He was the one who would delay Jacob for seven years as he was seeking for a wife, and then find a way of adding seven years more (as we shall discover in a later story).

But the servant will not allow delay. 'I am about to go back' he says. The question is put to Rebekah personally and immediately. God the Holy Spirit often speaks to us directly and personally, and He wants an immediate answer. *'Today if you hear His voice do not harden your hearts.'* The Spirit does not delay. He goes away if He does not receive an answer.

Chapter 4

The Side-Effects of Blessing
(Genesis 25:1–18)

Genesis 25 is a chapter full of the side-effects of God's grace and mercy. When God blesses there is always an 'overflow' and there come other blessings besides the central ones.

1. **Abraham is given strength and virility in his old age**. Genesis 25:1–18 concludes the story of Abraham. Abraham takes another wife. Her name is Keturah (25:1). This may have been after the death of Sarah and was certainly after the birth of Isaac. In either case the word 'concubine' in 25:6 and 1 Chronicles 1:32 makes it clear that she would never be the senior wife in the story of the covenant to Abraham. Through her Abraham has another six sons (25:2). Genesis 25:3 traces the descent of one of them to the third generation, and 25:4 traces the descent of another son via Keturah.

At one point Abraham was thinking he would never have a son since he was too old (17:17). But when the miracle takes place and God visits Abraham and Sarah, they both 'received power' (see Hebrews 11:11). Abraham not only has one son but another six through Keturah! The miracle of Genesis 21 involved newness of strength and virility.[1]

2. **Abraham leaves a message to those who live after him**. The line in which the covenant-promises would go forward would be that of Isaac, so he inherited everything that belonged to Abraham at the time of Abraham's death (25:5). Yet he took responsibility for his other children and provided for them during his lifetime so that there should be no dispute at the time of his death (25:6).

19

Then he died as a very elderly man and *'full of years'*, that is *'thoroughly satisfied with life'* (25:7–8). He went to live with the people of God beyond the grave. (The phrase 'gathered to his people' must mean that. Only Sarah was buried at Machpelah.) The way he arranged his will and his burial testified to his faith that the covenant promises would continue.

3. **There is blessing for the 'non-elect' as well as for God's elect**. Isaac and Ishmael were reunited (25:9–10) but the special line of blessing continued with Isaac (25:11).

In between the major sections of Genesis dealing with Abraham (11:27–25:11), Jacob (25:19–35:29) and Joseph (37:2–50:20), there are smaller sections dealing with Ishmael (25:12–18) and Esau (36:1–37:1). Genesis 25:12–18 looks briefly at Ishmael before continuing the story.

Ishmael is 'non-elect' as the heir of the covenant. It is Isaac who is chosen to be the bearer of the 'holy line of descent' leading to Jesus. *'In Isaac shall your seed be called,'* said God. *'My covenant I will establish with Isaac.'* At this point God's 'predestination' is not predestination to salvation, but predestination to usefulness in the progress of the covenant.

There are two mistakes that can be made here. Those who believe strongly in biblical predestination tend to read predestination-to-salvation into the Genesis stories of Isaac and Ishmael, Jacob and Esau. But the 'predestination' of Isaac and Jacob is not to salvation but to covenant-usefulness.

On the other hand those who like to play down the biblical teaching of predestination (as we have it in Romans 9 and elsewhere) tend to see nothing except 'predestination-to-covenant-usefulness' in Romans 9. Actually it is 'predestination-to-covenant-usefulness' in Genesis; and it is 'predestination-to-salvation' in Romans 9! Paul takes the stories of Genesis which refer only to 'predestination-to-covenant-usefulness' and he reapplies the principle to matters of salvation. The theme of Romans 9–11 is clearly that of the salvation or non-salvation of Israel. Paul is taking the stories of Genesis and reapplying them. The interpretation of the stories in their original context does not determine what Paul means in Romans 9 because Paul is **reapplying** them.

This is an important matter for another reason. The fact that Ishmael and Esau are 'non-elect' in the matter of 'covenant-usefulness' does not mean that they were 'non-elect' personally. The fact that Paul uses them as an **illustration** of people not being chosen to salvation does not mean that **personally** they were rejected by God and I do not believe they were. Hagar also ought to be mentioned in this connection because in Genesis 16 Hagar is saved and wonderfully blessed by God, but in Galatians 4 Hagar is used as a picture of 'the flesh'. What a biblical character is in God's picture-language may be different from what that character is in and of himself. Ishmael is a model of being by-passed by God in one respect but he probably was not by-passed personally. Esau was a model of being by-passed by God in one respect but in the letter to the Hebrews I think he is an illustration of a Christian who is 'saved through fire'.

There is blessing for those who may *not* be chosen to special significance in the history of salvation. I do not suggest that anyone can experience salvation without faith, but one might not be 'elect' as an Abraham, a Paul, a John Calvin, or one might not be highly prominent in the story of God's church – but be 'elect' to salvation nevertheless.

One thing is certain. Even Hagar, Ishmael and Esau gained much from the 'overflow' of God's purpose in Abraham, Isaac and Jacob. And Isaiah 60:6 mentions Midian, Ephah and Sheba (tribes descending from Abraham via Keturah!) and says to Israel *'Your sons will come from afar'* (Isaiah 60:4). He says to them as well as to Israel *'Arise, shine; for your light has come, and the glory of the LORD has risen upon you.'* One day those outside the seed of Abraham will experience God's worldwide revival and in that way come to be within the seed of Abraham!

Note

1. Abraham was 100 years old when Isaac was born (21:5). Sarah was ten years younger (17:17). Sarah died when she was 127 years (23:1);

21

Abraham was 137 years old at the time. Abraham died when he was 175 years (25:7). Abraham outlived Sarah by 38 years. If Isaac married Rebekah about 3 years after his mother's death (Abraham – 140) then Abraham died 35 years after Isaac's marriage (see 25:20).

Chapter 5

A Twisted Character Chosen By God

(Genesis 25:19–34)

A new section of Genesis, starting in Genesis 25:19, focuses on the next person that God is going to use in bringing in His salvation, and that is Jacob. Although it is the 'account of Isaac' (25:19), the word 'account' refers to the 'offspring' of someone or something, and so it deals more with Jacob and Esau than with Isaac himself.

1. **Jacob was a man with a difficult personality**. His very name, Jacob, means 'someone who grasps hold of the heel' or (to put it simply) 'Grabber'. It turned out to be prophetic. Isaac married Rebekah. Like Sarah many years before, she was unable to have children (25:19–20). Isaac prays for Rebekah and she conceives (25:21). One part of husbandly responsibility is that of intercession. Rebekah was conscious of something unusual happening within her, and asks God about it (25:22). She gets an answer. The two children are the forefathers of two nations (25:23); the nations will be Israel and Edom. When the boys were born, Jacob was born grasping Esau's heel (25:24–26). He lived that way all of his life. He was a 'Grabber' by name and a 'Grabber' by nature.

Jacob was a very home-loving person. He was rather soft, and loved an easy life. He liked his home comforts. Esau liked hunting, but not Jacob. The story in Genesis jumps forward to the days when the two boys are young men. One loves hunting and is his father's favourite; the other loves home and is his mother's favourite (25:27–28).

Jacob has a crafty streak in his character. One day Esau comes in starving, and as he arrives Jacob happens to be cooking some stew (25:29–30). Esau asks for some, and Jacob uses the occasion to get for himself the birthright. *'Sell me the birthright,'* says Jacob, and he is careful to have it given to him as a matter of oath (25:31–34).

This is typical of Jacob. The 'birthright' is the privilege of being the leader of the family. Normally it would belong to the firstborn. In the case of Abraham, Isaac and Jacob the 'birthright' that is being handed down included the promise of worldwide blessing coming through the line of Abraham. In despising the birthright Esau is despising the privilege of being used by God to fulfil His purpose. Jacob, although a crafty character, is sufficiently interested in the things of God as to wish he was the son who would carry forward the purposes of God. When he found an opportunity, true to his name, he grabbed it from Esau. This was typical of Jacob. He was quick to get something for himself.

Jacob was a thinker rather than a doer. The stories of how he exploited Esau show him to be a quick thinker. When Esau came home starving Jacob was instantly ready to think how he could exploit the situation to his own advantage.

Temperament is something you are born with. It never changes completely. Each person has his own collection of strengths and weaknesses. Some people are more greedy, more ambitious by nature, than others. Some are born activists. Some are born with strong emotional tendencies. Some are born highly intelligent. Each person has his own temperamental problems. No one is a perfectly balanced character.

2. **Jacob had one thing working in his favour, which was that God was determined to have him and use him**. Do you have a character that you think is a disability? You say to yourself 'God would never use a person like me.' Jacob was not the kind of person you think God would choose. But God had determined that He would use Jacob. The on-going line leading to Jesus would run through Jacob. Crafty Jacob had been chosen by God!

He was chosen before he was born. His future was planned by God. His being chosen by God had nothing to do with anything good in him. He was not chosen because of his good works. He was not a better person than Esau. Had we known both boys we might have liked Esau more than Jacob. Jacob was not God's servant because he was born good. He was not hindered from being God's servant because he was born bad. The purpose of God was not thrown aside just because Jacob was such a weak and twisted character. God chose to have him, no matter what disabilities he might have.

If God ever uses you it is not because you are a good person by nature and you deserve to be used. If God ever uses you at all it will entirely from God's goodness and mercy. When Rebekah had conceived by one man, although he had not yet been born and had done nothing good or bad, God was determining to have and to use Jacob. Quite independently of what his weaknesses of character might be, God decided to have him and use him. God can use you, just as He used Jacob, taking no notice of what Jacob's character was. God can do this because of Jesus. Jesus is our substitute before God. God can take hold of crooked personalities because Jesus has died for us. God can use us despite our sins, because Jesus died for them.

If God uses you the way He used Jacob, it will have to be by God's grace. We can never stand before God because of how good we are! Your works do not come into it. Your weaknesses and sins do not come into it either, because God saves you by grace.

Of course, God will change you! God chooses Jacob just as he is with his twisted character, but God does not leave Jacob just as he is. God begins to work in Jacob's life. That is how you become the servant of God. It starts with God's grace. Our God is 'the God of Jacob', the God who comes to twisted characters and saves them by His grace.

Chapter 6

Overcoming in Faith
(Genesis 26:1–35)

The story of the book of Genesis is the story of a promise. First we have seen the **need** of the promise, in Genesis 1–11. Now we are looking at the **outworking** of the promise. Abraham was told that through him and his seed all the world would be blessed. Eventually God made the promise into an oath and now it is sure and certain that the promise will come to pass. However the fact that a sworn oath must come to pass does not predetermine that any one particular person must be blessed by God. God can still withhold the blessings that have been sworn and give them to the next generation. Each patriarch, Isaac, Jacob, Joseph, has to persist in faith. Isaac is a person to whom the promise has been given. *'In Isaac shall your seed be called into being,'* said God. But for him, too, it involves overcoming the conflicts and testings that come to the man or woman believing the promise.

Let us consider, first, the problems of faith.

1. There is **unsettlement**. There is a famine in the land. This had happened before in the life of Abraham and Abraham had gone to Egypt (Genesis 12:10–20). But that occasion had not turned out well for Abraham. Isaac is distressed by anxiety about his physical well-being. God appears to him and warns him not to go (26:1–5).

2. There is **fear for one's life**. Like Abraham he fears that his life might be in danger because some powerful figure might want Rebekah as his wife.

3. There is **proneness to sin**. As often happens, anxiety led to sin. Abraham had twice half-lied about Sarah's being his sister. It was true that he and Sarah had the same father (see Genesis 20:12). On neither occasion had it done Abraham any good. Yet Isaac does the same thing. He does not have the excuse that Abraham had; in no way can Rebekah be thought to be Isaac's sister. He goes to the same place as Abraham had once gone to, Gerar, and tells the same lie (26:6–7). Isaac gets caught just as Abraham had twice been caught out before. This time someone is looking through a window (26:8)! Like Abraham he is rebuked by the pagan king for his suspicions and his deceit (26:9–10). But Abimelech gives a command that Isaac is not to be harmed.

4. There is **strife**. Isaac was rich and getting richer (26:12–14a) but wealth brings its own problems with it, and Isaac was the object of Philistine envy (26:14) and that in turn led to resentment and malice. They were stopping up his water-wells that had been dug by Abraham (26:15). He moved elsewhere at Abimelech's request (26:16–17) but that did no good. Although he opened up fresh water from old wells (26:18–19), the herdsman were still in the mood to be quarrelsome (26:20). So bad was the strife the very place-name was changed to 'Esek' ('Strife'). Further attempts to find another area still met with no success (26:21) and only on a further move did there come any peace (26:22).

5. There is **the strain of delay**. God had promised Isaac the land just as He had promised it to Abraham. In fact, the promise was more secure because it had been sworn to Abraham. Although Isaac and his people were hoping to be *'fruitful in the land'* (26:22), their inheriting of any land at all was slow in happening.

6. There is **a problem in the family**. After the blessing of God's appearing (26:24–25), and the end of the strife when Abimelech proposed a covenant (26:26–31), and the discovering of fresh water (26:32–33), that was still not the end of their problems. Esau decided to marry two Hittite wives (26:34–35). He was not interested in going back to Haran.

He wanted his wife now! And he wanted two! It brought great distress to Isaac and Rebekah.

However, although there are the conflicts of faith, there are also **the remedies of faith**.

1. The greatest of them is **the guidance and the presence of God**. When Isaac is about to go to Egypt, a trip that will take him away from the promised land and might well lead to disaster, God appears to him and says *'Do not go down to Egypt'* (26:1–2). God does not always give us direct guidance but there are times when we need special help or when God's kingdom is in special danger and we find we have the leading or the restraining hand of God.

2. There are **the renewals of God's promises**. God repeats the promises that He had given many times before: *'I will be with you and bless you ... I will give all these lands ... I will establish the oath ... I will multiply your descendants ... by your seed all the nations ... shall be blessed'* (26:3–4). There is an extra phrase that has not appeared before: *'because Abraham obeyed me.'* The oath may be a reward for obedience, and it was that way with Abraham. The day came when Abraham was summoned to a high level of obedience (17:1) and there was a day when God told Abraham that because of his fear of God he had received the oath (22:12, 16). For Abraham's sake God is renewing His promises to his seed.

3. There is **the forgiving grace of God**. Despite Isaac's foolishness (26:7–9), God had been gracious towards him. God showed him mercy in letting him be found out (26:10)! Sometimes God is merciful to us in letting us be exposed. Then God gave Abraham favour with Abimelech (26:11) and he was protected from the foolishness of his own ways.

4. **God added His blessing to Isaac's generosity**. Isaac was generous to the herdman. Several times he moved away. It is clear that he wanted to avoid strife if he could. God blessed him in his passivity and eventually even his enemy made peace with him. His patience was worthwhile and eventually he had the advantage of a covenant with Abimelech.

The life of faith brings many practical conflicts with it, but God is God and sees us through.

Chapter 7

Deceitful Ways; Painful Results

(Genesis 27:1–29)

God used one family in which to bring the Saviour, our Lord Jesus Christ, to the world. But at this point, the family of Abraham was not in a good condition.

Isaac had lost his spirituality. There had been a time when he would be meditating on the things of God and seeking His will. In Genesis 24:63 he was out in the fields seeking God at the time God answered his prayer and sent Rebekah to him. But now Isaac seems to be an unspiritual person. He likes his food more than he likes God's will. An occasion comes when Isaac thought he might not live very long and he wants to make a legal will handing over the leadership of the family to Esau (27:1–4). Isaac's eyesight was bad, and he was getting on in years. He wanted to legally 'bless' Esau before he died.

Now this 'blessing' was a very important matter. It was a way of handing over the supreme position of authority in the family. It meant that Isaac wanted Esau to have the privilege of managing the family property. And it meant that Isaac was expecting and praying that the worldwide 'blessing' that would come would take place through Esau. Isaac was taking no notice of the prophecy of Genesis 25:23 which said that *'the older shall serve the younger.'* His favourite son was Esau. He wanted the younger to serve the older! So he gets ready to legally make a 'will', a last 'testament' in which he legally handed over the leadership of the family to Esau.

Isaac gets ready to make this a special occasion. He calls only Esau, deliberately excluding Jacob. If he had not

29

excluded Jacob from the occasion Jacob would not have been able to play the trick that he did. Isaac ignored the prophecy Rebekah had received, and he ignored the legal oath with which Esau had sold his inheritance rights. It is clear that Isaac was not a very spiritual person at this time in his life. He had lost his love of God.

But **Rebekah is no better than Isaac**. Despite the great love which had once existed between Isaac and Rebekah (24:67) their relationship was no longer a close one. There was no communication between them. Rebekah's way of finding out what was happening was to listen to what Isaac said to other people (27:5)! They were not working together for the future of the family. Isaac was quite happy to plan his will without consulting Rebekah's wishes. Rebekah was quite happy to practise deliberate deception on her husband.

And **Jacob was not a very pleasant person**. We tend to treat him as one of the heroes of the Bible but at the beginning of his life he was not a very nice person to know. He did not begin as a godly person. God saves people by grace and not by 'good works'. It is a mistake to think that when God decides to use someone He chooses a godly person. Far from it. God chooses some very unstable, unsophisticated, unspiritual people, and then He shapes them to get them the way he wants them to be. Jacob was not a nice person or a godly person. Jesus said *'I have not come to save the righteous but to call sinners to repentance.'* If God can bless Jacob, God can bless me!

What a family. An unfair, pleasure-seeking father. A deceitful mother. A carnal-minded Esau. And a cheating, conniving, crafty Jacob!

Isaac asks Esau to prepare a meal (27:1–4). Rebekah and Jacob hear about what is happening, and they scheme to get things changed (27:5–8). While Esau is hunting for a animal to be a tasty dish for Isaac, Jacob prepares a meal. He dresses in Esau's clothes, and covers himself with some animal-skins so that he is like hairy Esau (27:9–17)!

The trick succeeds (27:18–29). He had to tell shameless lies and he even used pious spiritual language (27:20), but

Isaac was deceived and passed on the supremacy in the family to Jacob. *'May peoples serve you, and nations bow down to you. Be master of your brothers!'* he said as he legally passed the senior inheritance to his son (27:29)!

No one got much pleasure out of this event. **Isaac gained nothing worth having**. He had schemed to overthrow God's promise in Genesis 25:23. It was amazing that he should want to give the spiritual leadership of the family to someone who had just married two Hittite women and who cared nothing for the spiritual privileges of Abraham's line.

Rebekah gained nothing worth having. Her scheme created such resentment, Jacob had to run for his life, and she lost her favourite son. She had wanted to bring blessing into his life but actually she lost him altogether.

Jacob gained the inheritance but only at the price of great suffering. Jacob would have done better to leave his future in the hands of God. God had said that the elder would serve the younger. Jacob could have trusted God to bring about the promise.

The Bible says that there is a 'wisdom' that is earthly, natural or demonic (James 3:15). The cleverness of men and women is of no value in getting the blessings of God. You might even try to do God's will in deceitful ways but it will do no good.

The amazing thing was that God blessed Jacob anyway! Jacob's tricks brought him great suffering. Jacob had to run away. He lost his membership of the family altogether for many years. He never saw Rebekah again!

If God has promised blessing, He can be trusted to work it out for us. Our clever deceitful ways are not needed. God will give us His promise in a different way altogether. If we grab it prematurely, we shall only bring upon ourselves much delay and suffering.

Chapter 8

Human Folly, God's Mercy

(Genesis 27:30–28:9)

Isaac was unwilling to follow God's prediction concerning Jacob. Rebekah was manipulating her husband. Esau was ruining his life. Jacob was full of deceitful and tricky ways. Now the family fell into collective hatred, bitterness, remorse and mutual accusation.

Esau ruined his life by delayed interest in the rewards of God. Soon after Isaac had been deceived, Esau came in from his hunting trip (27:30). He spent some time preparing tasty food for Isaac and then, after Isaac had already given an unchangeable inheritance to Jacob, he came to Isaac. *'Sit up and have this nice meal I have prepared for you,'* he says (27:31), *'and then you will be able to give me your blessing'* (27:31). Isaac is shattered (27:32–33)! If this is Esau, who has he just given the blessing to? Deceitful Jacob! And it irreversible. *'Indeed he will be blessed!'* (27:33).

Esau cared nothing for the things of God. He had lived for his hunting and his belly. He had been a profane man, living life without reference to God.

Now he wants the blessing but he has lost it. It had been possible before to get the inheritance but now it was no longer possible. What made the loss irreversible was an oath. The New Testament says *'See that no one is sexually immoral or is godless like Esau, who for a single meal sold his inheritance rights as the oldest son. Afterwards, as you know, when he wanted to inherit this blessing, he was rejected. He could bring about no change of mind, though he sought the blessing with tears'* (Hebrews 12:17, NIV).

In the New Testament we have warnings against losing God's blessing. How shall we – as Christians – escape if we neglect the salvation we have and make no use of it? (see Hebrews 2:3). If we fall by the wayside an oath will be taken against us and we shall then not be able to get back to where we were before (see Hebrews 6:2–8). If God ever swears against us in anger an inheritance will be lost. Esau is a warning against the Christian who loses his reward because of carelessness.

The Christian might want the blessing that he was once careless about. Esau said *'Bless me, me as well as him, my father!'* (27:34). He had once been careless but now he wants the inheritance. But it is too late.

From one angle it was Jacob who, through Esau's carelessness, has tricked him. Yet Esau had to be responsible for his own life (27:35). An oath has been taken; nothing can be done to reverse it (27:36–37).

Esau weeps with distress (27:38). There comes a time when repentance is too late to bring about a change in the situation. Esau is repentant. He truly does now want this blessing and everything that is involved in it. But it is too late to bring a change in his father because a death-bed oath has been taken, and that cannot be changed. A Christian who loses his inheritance may be repentant. His repentance will restore his relationship to God but it will be too late to get back what has been lost. The Israelites who refused to go into Canaan wept when they heard that God would withhold the promised land from them. They mourned bitterly and confessed their sin (Numbers 14:40). And God really did forgive them (Numbers 14:20). Yet they lost something that they could not get back. When they said *'We shall go up to the place Yahweh promised'* (Numbers 14:40), Moses said that it was too late. *'You will be defeated'* (Numbers 14:42). Their distress could not bring back the lost opportunity. Their being forgiven secured their salvation; but the oath of God prevented them from getting back the reward they could have gotten for themselves.

The pattern is the same with Esau. His father loved him

33

still. He still got a word of prophecy from his father. But it was not much of a blessing. He and his people the Edomites would be subservient to Jacob. Only in the long-distance future would the people of Esau, the Edomites, throw off the yoke of Israelite dominance (27:39–40).

Jacob's deceit brought him exile and suffering. Because of the way in which Jacob had twice deceived him it is not surprising that Esau is exceedingly resentful about Jacob. He discovers Jacob has tricked him again (27:35) and says *'Is he not rightly named Jacob – Grabber, Trickster?'* and from that point onwards he hates Jacob (27:36). The animosity continues for a long time. *'Esau hated Jacob....'* Soon he was saying to himself *'I will kill my brother Jacob'* (27:41). Rebekah advises Jacob to run away (27:42–43). She thought it would not be long (*'Stay with him a few days,'* she says, 27:44). She fears she will lose both her sons (27:45). Poor Rebekah! Her life with Esau's Hittite wives is distressing her (27:46). She has another reason for sending Jacob to her brother Laban; she fears Jacob might follow Esau's example and marry a Hittite.

Jacob stayed with Laban for twenty years or so. Isaac agreed with the plan to send him away, and released him with words of good will (28:1–5). Esau clumsily tried to mend relationships with his parents by marrying a cousin who was not a Hittite (28:6–9). Eventually Esau got over his hatred of Jacob and was nice to him when they met twenty years later.

In the midst of failure God had mercy. When Jacob was sent away something happened to him on the journey. Jacob's deceit brought him exile and suffering, but as he is travelling God intervenes in his life in great kindness and graciousness. He reaches a certain place at nightfall and goes to sleep using a stone as a pillow. As he sleeps he is given a dream. It is a vision of God, and of God's mercy. The angels are coming down to meet him. God is still like this. When we have brought disaster upon ourselves by our foolish ways God is likely to have mercy.

Chapter 9

Jacob Have I Loved
(Genesis 28:10–22)

For many years Jacob had been stumbling through life with
his manipulative ways, but now God decided it was the time
to show Jacob mercy. We are all like Jacob really. We are
deceitful. We want our own way. We want to get things
arranged in such a way that they please us. We are self-
centred. And sometimes we make such a mess of our lives.
But when Jacob was helpless, hopeless, lonely, and facing
disaster, God stepped in.

Perhaps you are suffering from the consequences of your
own folly. You say 'If only I had not done that ... If only I
had not said that ... If only I had held on a bit longer...'.
The trouble comes from your own pride and self-centred-
ness. Yet that disastrous time in your life could turn out to
be a great time of blessing in your life.

1. **God uses a desperate occasion**. Jacob was disgraced in
the eyes of his family and must have been gripped with a
sense of failure. But it is precisely at such a time when we are
open to God. Jacob was just a self-centred character; it took
some suffering to get him to be willing to listen to what God
had to say.

2. **When God intervenes it is altogether a matter of mercy**.
Jacob leaves for Haran (28:10), and on the journey spends
a night sleeping in the open countryside (28:11). He uses a
stone as a pillow and while he is sleeping has a dream. In his
dream there is a staircase linking earth and heaven. Angels
are going up and down. In the dream, they are watching over

Jacob and bringing him the necessities he needs to survive the hazards of his journey (28:12). At the top of the staircase is Yahweh, the LORD Himself. In his dream God speaks to Jacob: '*I am Yahweh, the God of your father....*' The longstanding promise which God had given to Abraham, God now gives to Jacob. '*The land on which you lie, I will give it to you...*' (28:13).

Jacob must have thought that he had lost all hope of ever being '*Abraham's seed*'. He had tried manipulative ways to get the family inheritance. But now he was running away, and Esau was still back home close to Isaac and Rebekah. He was thinking that he had lost the inheritance for ever.

But no, God's original promise that He would use Jacob and that '*the older would serve the younger*' still holds true. God had never chosen Jacob because of how good he was. It was before he was born, and before he had done anything good or bad, that God announced '*The older will serve the younger.*' God gave the announcement before Jacob and Esau were born '*in order that God's purpose according to His choice might stand firm, not because of works but because of Him who calls...*' (Romans 9:11–12).

Now God was calling Jacob, summoning him into fellowship with Himself. It is clearly entirely a matter of mercy. It takes place at one of the worst times of Jacob's life!

Jacob is converted at this point, and is given the assurance that he will – despite all of his wickedness – be the one through whom the purpose of God will continue. It is he, not Esau, who will be the forefather of the nation of Israel.

'*In you and in your seed shall all the families of the earth be blessed*' (28:14). The promised 'Seed' will come through Jacob. '*I am with you...*', says God. '*I will watch over you wherever you go ... I will not leave you...*' (28:15).

3. **The promises of God concern both fellowship and future destiny**. God was ready to come down the staircase to meet Jacob and be with him for the rest of his life. (One recalls John 1:51. Jesus says He is the staircase! He is the one through whom the angels ascend and descend to care for God's people.)

But not only is there the promise of fellowship and salvation, God plans to use Jacob and the promises concern Jacob's destiny. God says His plan will go forward through Jacob. The divine and angelic presence will stay with Jacob until God has achieved all of His plans for and through Jacob.

4. **Purpose comes into Jacob's life when he responds to God**. He acknowledges that God has spoken to him (28:16–17). It is something he never wants to forget and so he takes the stone he has been using as a pillow and makes a small monument out of it to mark the spot where God spoke to him (28:18–19). He takes God at His word, and gives himself wholly to God (28:20–21). As a mark of his dedication to God he determines he will give a tenth of his income to God (28:22).

God still comes to us as we are in our sins, and He says 'I am willing to be with you, to use you, and never leave you, and get all My promises fulfilled through you.' This is why Jesus came. While we were yet sinners Christ died for us. We had not taken any steps to compensate for our sins. God stepped into the history of the human race.

You cannot do anything to save yourself. God has to step into your life. It does not matter how badly you have been living; God is willing to change things. Come to God. God says to you 'You have damaged your life, but out of the sheer love of My heart I will give Jesus to you. I will never leave you or forsake you. I will fulfil everyone of My purposes that I have for your life.'

'The Lord Almighty is with us; the God of Jacob is our refuge' (Psalm 46:7, 11). God is still the God of Jacob. He is the God of sinners, deceivers, manipulators. He comes to us when we have sinned, when we have damaged relationships. And He brings a change in our lives.

Chapter 10

The Deceiver Gets Deceived
(Genesis 29:1–20)

God has a lot of training to do in Jacob's life. This is the way it is with all of us. God saves us by His Son, our Lord Jesus Christ, but that is only the beginning. Jacob's conversion did not deliver him overnight from all of his bad habits and crooked ways. **He is now a man under the training of God**.

In Genesis 29 we are looking at some of the tough training programme that God had for Jacob.

For a while everything is made smooth for Jacob. He travels towards Haran and arrives at a well near Haran (29:1); we remember that Abraham's servant had found Rebekah at a spring near Haran. History is repeating itself. It is a place where there is a large stone for protecting the well which was used to water the sheep (29:2–3). It turns out that the shepherds are from Haran and that they know Laban, Jacob's uncle (29:4–5). Jacob's cousin Rachel is just about to arrive (29:6). The shepherds are having some difficulty rolling away the large stone covering the water-well (29:7–8).

Then Rachel appears (29:9) – just as her aunt Rebekah had arrived at the spring many years before. Rachel is a very attractive girl (see 29:17) and Jacob is immediately drawn to her. He pretends he has not seen her and does not know who she is (although he been told she is about to arrive and he does know who she is!). *'When Jacob saw Rachel ... Jacob went up, and rolled the stone from the mouth of the well'* (29:10). He wants her to see what a wonderful guy she has in her cousin Jacob! What a dashing, strong, helpful man he is

– when Rachel is watching! He removes the stone before he greets Rachel, although it would be normal to greet someone before you do anything else. Then he goes over to greet her and tell her who he is (29:11–12). He is pretending he was involved in rolling away the stone before she arrived! He is still the crafty Jacob, and is trying to impress her!

Rachel is also drawn to Jacob instantly, and runs excitedly to tell her father about the new arrival (29:13). Laban welcomes him warmly (29:14) and Jacob stays with these members of his extended family. Soon he has been there for a month. During that time he sees Rachel every day. He is also giving uncle Laban a lot of help, working with the sheep.

Laban is a crafty, greedy man. We have already noticed how he was attracted to the gold that Abraham's servant brought (*'When he saw the ring and the bracelets ... he said "Come in, blessed of the Lord..." '*, Genesis 24:30–31). He is even more deceitful than Jacob! Jacob does not know it but he is meeting someone who is even more of a trickster than he is!

God often disciplines us through a very intense need in our lives. Sometimes it happens when we fall in love! We find ourselves in a position where there is something and someone we want more than anything in the world. And that kind of situation produces in us an intense desire to get God to help us. We start praying as we have never prayed before. It might not be falling in love; it might be something else. It could be that we live in a country where education is not easily available and more than anything else in the world we want to go to school (Westerners might find that hard to understand!)

It might be that we are desperately poor and that we want to increase our social status. We see people who are wealthier than we are and we desperately want to pull ourselves up to their level. At such a time we would do anything to get God to help. There is no atheism in poor countries! People who are desperate discover that God is real.

God trains Jacob by letting him meet his own sins in someone else. If we do not deal with the way we are making others suffer, God is likely to let someone start treating us the way we have been treating others. Jacob has been tricking Esau out of his inheritance. He is known for his grabbing ways. Now, more than anything in the world, he wants Rachel – and now Laban starts outwitting him! Jacob, 'the Grabber', gets grabbed. The trickster gets tricked. Jacob has met his match and is now dealing with someone who is even more crafty than he is!

Laban knows a good catch when he sees one, and starts exploiting Jacob. 'I ought to pay you,' he says. 'Tell me what you would like for your wages' (see 29:15). Poor gullible Jacob! The deceiver is being deceived. Laban has two daughters but the one Jacob loves is the good-looking one, Rachel (29:16–18). 'Well', says Jacob, 'I love your daughter Rachel and want to marry her. You give me my basic living, and agree to let me have your daughter as my wife without any further dowry having to be paid, and I will agree to a contract of seven years' work' (29:19). Laban is getting a good bargain – and he has plans to make it even better. But he acts quite half-heartedly. He does not want Jacob to know what he really thinks. 'Better she marries you than someone else,' he says casually (29:20).

The fact is Jacob is meeting up with his own sinful ways by having to face them in someone else! Soon he will know what Esau felt like when he was tricked out of something that was precious to him. It is almost 'an eye for an eye, a tooth for a tooth'. Jacob is being made to see how despicable his tricky ways are. It is all part of the training of God for his life.

Chapter 11

Prepared For Usefulness

(Genesis 29:21–35)

Jacob is now a disciple, a learner. God is his teacher. He is coming under the discipline of many trials (29:1–30:43) and then will be made to face the painful truth about himself as never before (31:1–55). His painful training starts when there comes a very intense need in his life. He wants to marry Rachel. Then God trains Jacob by letting him meet his own sins in someone else.

The story jumps over seven years. Jacob finishes his contract for seven years' work and claims the fulfilment of his agreement (29:21). Laban agrees and arranges for a wedding festival (29:22). One gets the impression that there is not a good relationship between Laban and Jacob. The request for his wife has to come from Jacob. He has to 'remind' Laban of the agreement. The words of Genesis 29:21, *'Give me my wife,'* are short and sharp. Normally celebrations like this would take a whole week (if Judges 14:12–18 is a glimpse of normal practice). However the bride was to be given to the man on the night of the first day of celebrations. It was also the custom that the bride was to be veiled before her prospective husband until the night of the wedding (note what happens when Isaac and Rebekah first meet in 24:65). The wedding night was spent in a dark tent. Jacob was vulnerable to all of Laban's trickery. Late in the night Laban substituted Leah instead of Rachel (29:23). Her wedding-gift from her father is her maid Zilpah (29:24). In the darkness of the wedding-tent Jacob was deceived by

Leah also. When he woke up in the morning it was to discover that he had spent the night with Leah!

Jacob went through the kind of anguish that he had put Esau through. Over seven years previously Esau had wept in distress at being tricked by Jacob and had *'cried out with an exceedingly great and bitter cry'* (27:34). Jacob is now going through the same experience. Seven years before Jacob had deceived Isaac when *'his eyes were too dim to see'* (27:1). Now Laban has deceived Jacob when Jacob's eyes are dimmed by the lateness of the night and the veil which covers Leah's face. In a different way *'his eyes were too dim to see'* and he is being treated in the way in which he had treated his brother. Seven years before Rebekah had got Jacob to cooperate in deceiving Isaac; now Laban has got Leah to cooperate in deceiving Jacob. Seven years before once the oath was taken the situation could not be changed. Now, Jacob has fulfilled the marriage procedures with Leah. His situation cannot be changed and Leah is his for life! **God trains Jacob by letting him meet his own sins in someone else**.

After a protest from Jacob (29:25) and a feeble excuse from Laban (29:26), Jacob has to agree to another seven-year agreement to work for Laban. There was not much he could do. He was a long way from home. Normally in a situation of such injustice one would call upon one's family to help, but Jacob was in no position to ask the help of Isaac and Esau! He has to 'celebrate' his marriage to Leah for seven days (29:27) and then he is given Rachel as his second wife seven days after marrying his first wife (29:28). She too is given a wedding-gift, her maid Bilhah (29:29).

Training can come when we are forced to handle strife and conflict. Jacob is happy to have his beloved Rachel (29:30) but he has also collected a whole host of troubles for himself. He is now committed to another seven years working for Laban. He has two wives, but one of them he does not love. Inevitably there will be rivalry and jealousy between the two sisters. Jacob had behaved badly in a situation of rivalry with his brother; now he has to cope with rivalry between two sisters and he is married to both of them! He had stolen the position of Isaac's beloved Esau; now Laban has arranged things so that Leah stole the position of his beloved Rachel.

However there are three ways in which God is overrules in all of this. (1) It gives Jacob a forced understanding of what his own character is like. He meets his own sins in the sins of others. (2) Despite the great pain of what is happening to him it actually advances the promises of God. God had promised to multiply the family of Abraham and especially do so through Isaac and through Jacob. Of the eight tribes that came out of Jacob's line, eight of them descended from Leah and her maid Zilpah. (3) Meanwhile God softened the pain for Jacob by giving him his beloved Rachel, and he softened the great pain of the unloved Leah by giving her four children (29:31–35). It would at least give her a position of honour in the family. God knows how to adjust pains and joys, so that the joys enable us to keep our peacefulness in the midst of troubles.

When we have a deceitful character as Jacob did – and we are all Jacobs in one way or another – God has to take the surgical knife to us. Troubles and strife of one kind or another will drive us to God. The very worst aspects of our character are likely to be forced to the surface so that we see ourselves as we really are.

God still uses us. Jacob was chosen, we remember, before he was born. His future was planned by God. His being chosen by God had nothing to do with anything good in him. He was not a better person than Esau.

We are saved without works and God starts using us without regard for our goodness or our wickedness. And yet God does want our character to change. And the greatest blessings are likely to come when we have become *'a vessel for honour, sanctified, useful to the Master'* (2 Timothy 2:21).

Chapter 12

Persistence Amidst Many Worries

(Genesis 30:1–24)

Rachel has got the desire of her heart – Jacob. But now there is something that brings her great distress. Like Rebekah and Sarah before her she finds that she cannot have children easily.

One part of the discipline of God is to teach us how to endure and overcome amidst quarrels and conflicts. At this stage of Jacob's life he comes under the most awful pressure. It is not so much a matter of danger to his life – although that will soon come as well. At first it is more the sheer ugly pressure that comes when a host of criticisms and quarrels thrust themselves upon us.

First there is a damaged relationship with Rachel that arises because of her childlessness. She seems to be blaming Jacob. *'Give me children, or else I die,'* she says (30:1). It is a most unreasonable way of expressing her problem.

There is one thing that is worse than having an enemy, and that is to have an enemy that one cannot reason with. What is the point of any kind of discussion with a childless wife who says *'Give me children, or else I die'*? One can discuss an intelligent complaint, but not one put in the way Rachel puts it. Jacob does not react well – and nor would we. He is simply angry (30:2); an unreasonable illogical critic is extremely infuriating. It tests Jacob to the limit of his self-control and he does not stand up well to the test.

Yet **facing unreasonable criticism** is part of God's training and testing him. God wants us to get to the point where we can take the most unreasonable accusations and stay cool. It takes some of us a long time to get there. Jesus is our model. Amidst the most infuriating false accusations, He was able to keep silent (Mark 14:61). When falsely accused He did not hurl back counter accusations. He did not return *'evil for evil, or insult for insult'* (1 Peter 3:9). God wants us to be Christ-like in this respect, and there is no way we can ever get to be like Jesus unless we are put into situations of false accusation sometimes even from those who are nearest and dearest to us.

Amidst such pressure, Jacob has to face temptations to act impulsively. Years ago Abraham had been in a similar situation and he had turned to Hagar in order to get a son. It was a piece of worldly manipulation, and it did Abraham no good. It certainly did not hasten the birth of Isaac. Soon Rachel turns to the same remedy that Sarah had turned to years before, and suggests that her maid should be used to produce children for adoption (30:3–4).

It was possible among the pagans of those days for a man with a childless wife to make use of a slave-girl in order to produce a child. In such a situation the childless wife took the child as her own and the true mother had no rights in the matter. It had brought no blessing to Abraham, Sarah, Hagar, Ishmael or Isaac, but we always seem to feel that we can make sin turn out good, even though no one else can! Bilhah gave birth to Dan (30:5) which Rachel treated as her own (30:6). Then a second son was born, Naphtali (30:7–8). Leah seemed to be having a similar problem. She demanded that Jacob should have more children by Zilpah; two more children were born (30:9–13).

It would soon teach Jacob that it was not the way to get God's will done. It would not lead to peace or happiness however much God might overrule it.

Rachel was still desperate to have children of her own. Mandrakes were thought to promote fertility and so Rachel begged Leah for her mandrakes; Leah made use of the occasion to hire Jacob for the night ((30:14–16)! The result was a fifth son for Leah (30:17–18) and later a sixth (30:19–20) and then a daughter (30:21).

The point of all of this is that Jacob was living in an atmosphere of intense jealousy, rivalry and quarrelsomeness. Even the sight of a few mandrakes in the hands of Leah was enough to make Rachel jealous and sneaky. Jacob has four wives who are wrangling for the privilege of his company. Two of them are ex-servant-girls desperate to find some respect and affection. One of them is an unloved wife. Another is a wife who has no self-respect because she has had no children. In the midst of it all is Jacob, who is at the mercy of these women arranging between themselves who has him for the night.

Jacob learns that a prayer delayed is not a prayer denied. At long, long last Rachel herself gave birth to Joseph (30:22–24). It was what Jacob and Rachel had wanted for many years. Rachel had long given up and had turned to all sorts of desperate remedies. She was thinking that there was no likelihood that this prayer would ever be answered. And yet it was. We should learn never to give up praying for something that is good and right. Unless God clearly says 'No' He wants us to persevere in our praying and not give up. He may answer at an unexpected time. Or He may answer in a different manner from what we were anticipating.

But **the greatest lesson** that Jacob must learn **is that of persisting under pressure**. Four desperate women are causing him anxiety and strain. An employer who is oppressive and dishonest is haggling over his work with the sheep and goats. Children from four different mothers would all have their own rivalries and discords. And yet Jacob has to keep a cool head. His life is not all about women, and conflicts, and uncertain payments from a domineering employer. Jacob's life is about the promises of God. Where is the promise of Canaan in all of this? Where is the promise of land to be inherited and worldwide blessing for all nations? It is this that Jacob has to keep as the centre of his aspirations and hopes. He had once acknowledged that God had spoken to him (28:16–17). He had given himself wholly to God (28:20–21). He had determined to give God a tenth of his income

(28:22). Now amidst a host of conflicts and responsibilities the question is: will he get *'choked with worries'* (Luke 8:14), or will he persist in inheriting the promises of God?

Chapter 13

New Ventures in Faith

(Genesis 30:25–31:16)

Jacob is now wanting to be released from Laban (30:25–26). He had only intended to go to Haran for a short time, but he has stayed for well over twenty years. He now has four wives, eleven sons and at least one daughter. God had told him many years ago that He would bring Jacob back to the land of Canaan, and now that Jacob has a son through his favourite wife he wants to go back home to settle. He is hoping that the troubles with Esau will now have ceased. He has not seen Esau for twenty years and he hopes that by now Esau's murderous intentions will have fallen aside. Yet there are some things he has to get clear before God will allow him to go home. At this point Jacob is learning new lessons in faith. He is not a great man of faith; so far he has been more of a manipulator than a believer. But God wants him to grow in faith before he goes home.

The offer of a rise in wages tempts Jacob to stay longer. Laban has profited from Jacob and is not eager to lose his easily manipulated worker. He presses Jacob to stay on (30:27–30). But Jacob is ready to learn some things he never realised before.

1. **Jacob follows the instinct of his faith**. Jacob agrees to stay on if he will be allowed to take the spotted and speckled goats and lambs. Laban will have the animals which are uniformly one colour, while Jacob will take the smaller number that are spotted and speckled (30:31–33). It is a difficult suggestion to refuse. The sheep are mainly all white. The goats are mainly all brown or black. Laban agrees, but

48

is soon playing his old tricks and removes the sheep that would belong to Jacob. He is still determined to exploit Jacob as much as he can (30:34–36).

What we have here is what I would call an 'intuition of faith'. Sometimes faith has to follow a kind of instinct. The Bible has many examples. Abraham's feeling that he should find a wife for Isaac in Haran was an example. 1 Samuel 14:6–14 is another example. Jonathan said *'Let's go ... Perhaps the Lord will act ... '* (1 Samuel 14:6). He was not 100% sure but it seemed to him that that was the way God was leading him. Jacob felt he had to trust God to work for him in a way that would make it quite clear that God was at work.

It was a step forward for Jacob. It is a rare event in Jacob's life for him to be trusting God rather than manipulating. Jacob was taking a step towards a greater trust in God. He is making an arrangement the results of which will depend on whether God lets speckled and spotted sheep and goats get born in large numbers.

2. **Jacob is letting God do the manipulating**. He is willing to leave the matter entirely in the hands of God. The speckled and spotted animals will be his wages. *'My honesty will testify for me in the future,'* he says (30:33). This is a gigantic step forward for Jacob. Never before has he ever said 'My honesty will testify for me'! Normally he has been the very opposite of honest; he has spent a lifetime in deceit. Laban removes all the speckled and spotted animals to start with, so what chance does Jacob have to make much profit? Jacob follows his intuition. He lets the flocks of sheep and goats mate in the sight of patchy rods of wood (30:37–43). There is no known technique for producing patchy animals in this way. It was probably just a representation of what he was trusting would happen. But since Jacob was trusting God, God honoured him and allowed the odd scheme to work!

Jacob also kept strong and weak animals separate and only let the strong ones see the multicoloured posts of wood; so the strong ones were patchy and the weak ones were of one colour (30:42).

Whatever the scientific procedure might be, it worked! Soon Jacob grew prosperous with multicoloured flocks of sheep and goats. The lesson he was learning is that trusting God is better than manipulation. Manipulation does not allow anyone to say *'My honesty will testify for me.'*

3. **Laban's deceit fails**. The herds of Laban are now small, and the animals are weak. Laban's sons began to get resentful and to accuse Jacob of stealing from Jacob (31:1). Laban himself becomes even more unfriendly (31:2).

It is all a demonstration to Laban and to Jacob himself, that manipulation is not necessary, and that faith and honesty are the best policy. A weak strand in Jacob's character – his deceitfulness – is being thoroughly challenged.

Jacob is now ready to go home. And God is ready too. The great sin of Jacob which made him run from Canaan in the first place has been overcome on at least one occasion. Jacob never will be entirely free of it, and he shows his old deceitfulness even in the way in which he leaves Laban. But at least he has made a start. He has learned on at least one occasion that honesty is best. God is willing now that the call of Jacob's life should go forward, and that calling concerns Canaan not Haran.

Soon God appears to Jacob and tells him to return (31:3). Jacob explains the situation to his wives (31:4–13) and tells them the story of how God has appeared to him. The wives do not reckon they any longer have a place in Laban's affections; they are ready to leave (31:14–16). More than twenty years training has gone by for Jacob. This is God's way. Some of us get quite old before the greatest work of our life appears before us. We need a long time, perhaps decades, before we get to the position of faith and purity and openness. When we get to that point the calling of our life begins to move forward more speedily.

Chapter 14

Discovering Ourselves
(Genesis 31:17–32:8)

Jacob is still in the process of discovering himself. For a long time he has been a man of deceit and trickery but he is slow to recognize this deceit in himself. Jacob is a disciple, a learner. God is his teacher. He has come under the discipline of various trials (29:1–30:43) and is now being made to face the painful truth about himself (31:1–55).

1. **Again he is taught that evasiveness does not pay**. Jacob leaves Laban. There is still a lot of evasiveness in his character. He makes no attempts to explain anything to Laban; he simply leaves (31:17–18). At the same time Rachel steals the idols that Laban had at home; they seem to have had value as an entitlement to the family inheritance [1] (31:19). Jacob's way of acting lacks any kind of frankness. *'Jacob deceived Laban'* says Genesis 31:20. When Laban found out he was furious and soon started to pursue Jacob's family. Jacob is in Canaan by the time Laban catches him, in Gilead (31:21–23). Laban is ready to do harm to Jacob but God warns him in a dream to leave Jacob alone (31:24). So he catches up with the fleeing family (31:25) and complains bitterly to Jacob (31:26–28), telling him of how he was inclined to do him harm (31:29) and complaining about the stolen gods (31:30). Jacob once again is discovering that God will not bless any of his efforts at self-centred manipulation. Not a single piece of deceit has turned out good since he was a young man. The only successful venture in his life has been the time when he said 'My honesty will answer for me.'

51

2. **Jacob tells of his fear** (31:31). It is an important confession. Behind Jacob's deceitfulness is fear. And behind fear is unbelief and lack of love. Faith works by love (Galatians 5:6). Love throws out fear (1 John 4:18). Weak faith produces flimsy love. Inadequate love is full of fear. Fear leads to deceit.

Jacob swears no one has stolen Laban's gods (31:31); he does not know about his wife's theft (31:32). But Laban's search does no good (31:33) and Rachel's trickery is as good as her father's (31:34–35) and her husband's. Jacob is in a position to act self-righteously as though he were a model of good behaviour (31:36–37). He certainly can claim that Laban has had a good bargain in having had Jacob to work for him (31:38–41) and that only God's protection of Jacob has preserved him (31:42). Laban is still self-justifying (31:43) but suggests they part peaceably (31:43). The two make a covenant (31:44–46) with a stone monument as a witness which they call 'The heap of witness' in Aramaic and in Hebrew (31:47–55). Then they separate peacefully.

3. **The past begins to catch up with Jacob**. The angels of God are travelling with Jacob (32:1), and Jacob sends messengers ahead to tell of his coming (32:2–5). But soon he has a piece of frightening news. Esau is coming to meet him and has four hundred men with him (32:6). Jacob is afraid. The last time he had any contact with Esau, Esau was threatening to kill him. Now Esau is travelling towards Jacob with four hundred men! It is the greatest danger Jacob has been in since he ran from Esau over twenty years ago. What will he do now? It is a sin of the past catching up with him. He had never dealt straightforwardly with the complaints of Esau. He had simply run for his life without caring to reach any happy arrangement with Esau. Now Esau is on his way with a large number of men, almost an army!

God was encouraging Jacob to deal boldly with the past. The warning to Laban (31:24) and the accompanying angels (32:1) were indications that God was with him. He had made peace with Laban. Now is the time to become reconciled to

Esau. He knows that God is with him. He calls the name of the place 'Mahanaim' – 'Two Camps'. Alongside his own camp there is a host of angels. God who sent angels to protect him when he was travelling to Haran (28:12) is now sending angels to protect him on his return.

But not even an angelic army is enough to make Jacob trust God alone. He has to do some organising himself! He divides his large company into two (32:7). At least half might survive if Esau invades (32:8). He still needs to make his own arrangements as well as having God's angels. Apparently Jacob feels the angels could do with some practical scheming to help them along with their protective measures!

In all of this Jacob is being forced to discover himself. He should have learnt by now that treacherous subterfuge and sneaky dishonesty simply brought no blessing to him. Had it worked with Esau? With Isaac? With Laban? And the cause of the whole business is still not dealt with. The violent hostility of Esau over twenty years ago was caused by Jacob. One might think it would fall aside with the passing of all these years. Jacob's past wickedness has caught up with him.

Many of us have to come to the point where we are forced to face ourselves and our personal weaknesses. Jacob has reached that point. All he can do now is pray.

So in his desperation Jacob turns to God. It is this that God wants. A man who is desperate is open to God's ways and God's will. Perhaps Jacob will get rid of his trickery and deceit for ever. Jacob's only hope, in his extreme desperation, is that the God of Abraham and the God of Isaac will come to his rescue. When we discover ourselves and see the awful truth, we are getting close to discovering God and His great mercy.

Note

1. This is based on a similar custom at Nuzi. It has been disputed but still remains the best explanation, in my opinion.

Chapter 15

Seeking Reconciliation

(Genesis 32:9–21)

Jacob has been made to face the painful truth about himself (31:1–55). He now is driven to a point of desperation where God performs some radical surgery in his life (32:1–32).

It begins when Jacob, greatly afraid of what is to happen when he meets with Esau, turns to God in prayer. He is afraid for his life, and yet he was reaching the point where he did not want to make use of deceit and trickery any more. What can he do? He can pray! **He considers what God has done in days gone by**. God has a good reputation with Jacob. Jacob knows how God greatly blessed Abraham and Isaac. Despite all of their weaknesses, he knows that God has been *'the God of ... Abraham, the God of ... Isaac'* (32:9). If we have eyes to see, we see how gracious God has been to our predecessors. We are no better than them, but then they were no better than us. Many of the great heroes of the past were as weak as we are. If God helped them, God can help us. It affects the way Jacob prays. *'God of Abraham ... God of Isaac ... '*, he says.

He considers God's instructions and God's promises. *'O Lord who said to me "Return to your country and to your family, and I will do you good." '* It was God who had told him to return to Canaan. Jacob feels he can hand his distressing situation over to God. God is responsible for it; He can be trusted to handle it.

He confesses his unworthiness. This is a new note in the story of Jacob. Hitherto he has deceived everyone and never has admitted to having much need in his life. But now things are different. '*I am not worthy of the least of your mercies* ... ', he says (32:10). He is looking back over his life. Years ago he was a lonely refugee, fleeing from the wrath of Esau his brother. Now he has two large companies of people. He has become a respectable family man and has acquired considerable wealth. It is all due to God and His mercy. Jacob uses this as an argument in prayer. If God has been so good to him in days gone by, will God not be good to him now?

He puts his request to God. '*Deliver me ... from the hand of my brother* ... ' (32:11).

He ends his prayer clinging to the promises of God about his future. God had told him he would become as many as the grains of sand on the seashore. How can he become as the sand on the seashore if Esau wipes out his wives and children? (32:11).

After he has prayed he does what he can to turn aside the anger of Esau. He sends gifts ahead (32:13–20). His servants are to say to Esau '*He is behind us.*' The servants must make it quite clear that Jacob is on his way to meet Esau face-to-face. There is to be no sneaking around Esau as there had been as evasive avoidance of Laban. Jacob is determined to face Esau in an open and straightforward way. He sends the propitiating sacrifice ahead and then he hopes to meet Esau face-to-face.

One can hardly pass by a passage like this without noticing how it illustrates what it means to pray by means of the blood of Jesus. It is only an illustration, and not a perfect one. The Bible says that Jesus is the 'propitiation' for our sins, and the word 'propitiation' means a sacrifice that turns aside wrath. Our passage beautifully illustrates the idea. Esau was angry with Jacob. Jacob sends an expensive and costly gift ahead hoping to turn aside Esau's wrath. '*I may appease him with the present ... afterwards I shall see his face*' (33:20).

Of course the illustration is not perfect. Esau's wrath is bad temper and resentment. God's wrath is a matter of justice and righteousness. It is a determination to wipe sin out of existence. Jacob's gift is one of his own providing, but the blood of Jesus Christ is provided by God. But the essential idea of propitiation is illustrated for us here. God is angry with sin. We are not acceptable to Him as we are. There is only one way in which the anger of God against our sin can be turned away. We must send ahead of us the blood of Jesus Christ. God accepts the gift and then, through the blood of His Son, accepts us and we see and meet Him face-to-face. In Jacob's case it is reconciliation with his brother that he wants.

He has the courage to approach Esau looking for reconciliation. The idea has come from Jacob. Esau has not sent any friendly overtures to Jacob. It is the other way around. When there is disharmony and conflict, who should take the first step? We should! Our brother may not be interested in having reconciliation with us, but we are interested in having reconciliation with him. We are the ones who are to take the first step.

He takes extreme measures to persuade Esau to be friendly. He sends multitudes of animals. They arrive at Esau's camp one at a time, *'each drove by itself'* (32:16). First there are goats, then sheep, then camels, then cows, and then asses. With each of the five groups there are males to make sure that the size of Esau's flocks will increase. Five times Esau will hear the servants say *'They are a present ... he is behind us.'* Jacob is taking extreme measures to bring about reconciliation.

There is one more thing: he must wrestle with God and get God to answer his prayer. He cannot live on deceit and trickery any more. It is God or nothing; it is now or never. He is determined to get God's blessing on his life or perish in the attempt!

Chapter 16

Attacked By God

(Genesis 32:22–32)

As we have seen, Jacob is a naturally cunning and devious person. Through his experiences with Laban he has learned the folly of deceitfulness of character, although it has to be said that this aspect of his character has not been eradicated. On one occasion when Jacob had determined to trust God and act in honesty it had worked well. *'My honesty will answer for me,'* Jacob had said (30:33) and God had blessed him. But Jacob's experiment with honesty still had not greatly changed his character, and now he was in the greatest crisis of his life. He has left Laban and cannot possibly go back there. Yet he has also heard that Esau is about to meet him and has four hundred men with him. The last time Jacob was in touch with Esau, Esau had been threatening to kill him. Jacob is afraid (32:6–7).

Jacob does his best to take safety measures (32:7–8) and he prays (32:9–12). Then he sends gifts to Esau hoping that Esau's anger will be turned aside. But he has no idea how Esau will respond, and does not know what will happen. So far as he knows his life is still in great danger. He is being threatened with the loss of everything he has and the end of his life.

He comes to the Jabbok river. Over the other side of the river he can reckon he is in the land which God has promised to give to the seed of Abraham. God had promised to give that land to Jacob, but that happened more than twenty years previously and nothing of God's promises had ever been fulfilled during those twenty years.

Have you ever been in a critical situation, a time when it is 'now or never' in your life, a time where you hardly know whether you are facing life or death? Jacob is either going to come through this terrible time in his life or he is about to lose his life. The promises of God are either going to start going forward in the land God promised Jacob, or the promises are about to be forfeited altogether. The purpose of Jacob's life is either about to move forward or it is about to be aborted. The question is: which way are things going to go? Jacob does not know.

If he is to achieve God's purpose for his lifetime he must go to Canaan. He is now ready to renounce his under-handed, self-centred, self-reliant ways and begin to live on God. But if this is to happen he has to become reconciled with Esau.

1. **He arranges to be alone**. He sends his family ahead (32:21b–23). *'Jacob was left alone'* (32:24). Jacob knows that he must deal with God in a very personal way.

2. **God appears to him**. It is God who takes the initiative. It is always this way. At times when we are desperate God has a habit of stepping in. God appears to Jacob. A very tangible figure appears. Genesis 32:24 says *'A man wrestled with him till daybreak.'* There is a fight, which is real and which is physical. This is not an 'incarnation'; it is not like God's becoming man in Jesus. It is actually an angel. Yet the angel appears in human form, and the angel is representing God. It becomes clear that the figure is God (see 32:30). Hosea 12:3 and 4 say *'He struggled with God'* and *'He struggled with the angel.'* This 'angel' is not like a ghost or a 'spirit'. He has material form, and He starts wrestling with Jacob seeking to throw him to the ground. God has taken the initiative in dealing with Jacob.

3. **God fights with Jacob in a gentle way**. *'A man wrestled with him until daybreak'* (32:24) but the supernatural figure was not able to prevail against Jacob. What can this mean? Why is it that a supernatural figure representing God Himself is not able to defeat Jacob and throw him to the ground? God wrestles with Jacob all night, but He is not

successful! The reason must be that God is being more gentle than He could be. God is quite capable of immobilising Jacob at any time He likes. His method of fighting is gentle. He will defeat Jacob only if Jacob gives in.

The battle with Jacob is quite literal, yet at the same time it is a parable of the way in which God has been dealing with Jacob for many years. For over twenty years God has been fighting to get Jacob to change his character and become a new man in God. But God's way of fighting has been gentle. He has not been forcing Jacob to surrender his devious ways.

Jacob refuses to give in or admit defeat. He withstands his mysterious assailant. 'The man' will have to fight more aggressively if he is to win. The angel of God wishes not to be totally seen. He has visited Jacob at night in order to veil his appearance. As the first streaks of dawn appear God wishes to leave, but He has still not defeated Jacob. Jacob is not the kind of person who gives in easily! Throughout his life God has not been **breaking** Jacob in a violent way. He has been gentle. He has been **inviting** Jacob to admit defeat, abandon his manipulative ways, and let God be his leader, his guide, his vindicator. The literal fight is typical of the spiritual battle God has been having with Jacob for many years.

God is restraining Himself. God wants to change us, but it is possible for God to fight with us and not be winning! God wants our **willing** submission. He wants us to surrender to Him **without** His having to knock us down or injure us.

Chapter 17

A Happy Defeat
(Genesis 32:22–33:20)

As we have seen, the battle with Jacob is a parable of the way in which God has been dealing with Jacob for many years. God has been fighting to get Jacob to change his character and become a new man in God. But Jacob is not the kind of person who gives in easily!

4. **When God's gentle fighting does not succeed, He uses a more forceful method**. Jacob refuses to admit defeat. He withstands his mysterious enemy, and so 'the man' has to fight more aggressively. With supernatural power he touches Jacob's thigh and injures him. Jacob is defeated. Jacob is now aware – if he has not been aware before – that his mysterious attacker is a supernatural being. He knows that God has defeated him. God has increased the forcefulness of His ways with Jacob and is compelling Jacob to surrender.

This is what God can do to us if we will not yield to His ways willingly. God is being more forceful in getting Jacob to submit. Esau is ahead. Laban is behind. There is a river to cross. Jacob has to admit defeat and get God to bless him on God's conditions.

5. **Jacob is defeated but becomes more desperate than ever for God's blessing**. God now wants to go (32:26a) but Jacob needs God more than ever. He admits defeat. He admits that God can do anything with him and can immobilise him – or anyone else – with the slightest touch of His supernatural power. He now clings to the supernatural visitor and pleads for blessing. Even though he is wounded and crippled he

clings to the supernatural being. *'I will not let you go unless you bless me,'* he says (32:26b).

Jacob is surrendering to the heavenly visitor. He is defeated and crippled and yet he is insistent that he wants God's help and blessing in his life. This is how God wants us to be. He wants us to be ready for anything He might do to us, anything He might call us to. Jacob becomes open to God as never before. The angel asks Jacob to be honest. *'What is your name?'* Jacob's name is 'Twister' or 'Grabber'. For much of his lifetime Jacob has lived up to his name. Recently in his life he has been wrestling with the possibility of breaking free from his weakness and living more on God than upon his own manipulativeness. Now the angel challenges him: What is your name? What are you really like? What is your real character? (32:27a). Jacob is willing to give the answer. He knows that his name means 'Grabber', 'Grasper', 'One Who Grabs People By the Heel'. That is exactly who he is and exactly the way he has been living all of his life. Now he is willing to admit that he is who he is. He confesses that he is 'Grasper' by name, and 'Grasper' by nature (32:27b).

6. **Jacob gets victory by being defeated by God**. Now that Jacob has given in, and surrendered to God, God is ready to come to his help and answer his prayers. *'Your name shall no longer be Jacob, Grasper,'* says God (32:28). From now on Jacob will have the name and the character of 'Israel'. The word-play in the name is obscure but the following words – 'for you have fought with God and with men and have prevailed' – make it clear that the sense is 'Fighter With God'.

Jacob has fought with God and has won by being defeated! God is now going to help him. The promises given to Jacob long ago are to go ahead. God will allow Jacob to cross the river Jabbok and enter the promised land.

Jacob has also fought with men and prevailed. God is about to bless Jacob's endeavours at reconciliation with Esau. All of his life Jacob has been striving to get advantage over others. Now he has been striving for reconciliation.

Jacob knows he has entered into a deeper fellowship with God. He says to the supernatural figure *'Please tell me your name'* (32:29). He know that his mysterious attacker is a supernatural being. He suspects that the attacker is God Himself! God has increased the forcefulness of His ways with Jacob and forced Jacob to surrender.

God will not reveal His name. The full revelation of God's name will come in the days of Moses, when God reveals the meaning of 'Yahweh' – the God who redeems His people by the blood of the lamb. But God does bless Jacob. He reveals Himself as the one who defeats us in order to bless us.

Jacob names the place 'Peniel', *'the face of God'* (32:30). Jacob knows now that he has experienced a revelation of God, in an amazing way. It was only a partial revelation. It took place at night. The angel left before dawn. Yet Jacob knows that he has met with God.

7. **Jacob is made to know that he must spend the rest of his life as one who leans on the help of God**. He crosses Jabbok limping (32:31). He will never be allowed to be his old self again. From now on he will be crippled and will have to look to God to give him special help. What happened on that night must be the way he lives for the rest of his life. From now on he must be one who knows his own weakness and trusts in the strength of God.

8. **This way of living must be learnt by the nation of Israel**. It became a custom not to eat meat that came from the hip of an animal (32:32). Jacob – or Israel as he is now called – insists that his people remember what has happened to him. For the future nation of Israel must live as their forefather lived. They must be a people who know their own helplessness but have learned to live in dependence on God.

9. **God abundantly answers Jacob's wish for reconciliation**. Genesis 33 is the end of the story of Genesis 32. It tells of the results of Jacob's new surrender to God. Jacob's desire for reconciliation to Esau is fulfilled. Somewhere in his journey Esau's attitude had been completely changed. Jacob had fought with men (see 32:28) as well as with God! He had

striven for reconciliation with his brother and he won a victory of love.

Jacob sees Esau coming. He puts those members of the family that he values least in the front. Leah the next most favoured is in a second group. The most favoured members of the family are put in the safest position (33:1–2). Favouritism was a mark of all the patriarchs! God's people have not reached New Testament standards of wisdom.

Jacob himself goes ahead of his family. He is extremely courteous towards Esau, and acts in a very apologetic manner. It is Jacob's way of seeking to make amends for his horrid treatment of his brother in years gone by (33:3).

But God has answered his prayers. Esau who came with a large number of men welcomes Esau (33:4), and there is a happy family reunion in which Jacob introduces his wives and children (33:5–7). Jacob explains he wants Esau's favour and forgiveness (33:8), and insists that Esau takes his gifts (33:9–11).

Esau wants to travel with his brother (33:12) but Jacob asks to be allowed to travel more slowly with his family (33:13–14) and will meet Esau at Seir (33:13–14). He is promising that he will visit Esau later. Esau offers further help but it is not needed and Esau leaves (33:15–16). Jacob travels on, making a dwelling-place at Succoth (33:17) but buying land in Shechem (33:18–19), where he builds an altar, calling it *'God, the God of Israel'* (33:20; the word 'Israel' in the name of the altar refers to Jacob not to the nation). In a greater way than ever Jacob knows that God is his God.

Chapter 18

Re-Discovering God
(Genesis 34:1–35:11)

Israel (as Jacob is now called) has received a wonderful answer to his desire for reconciliation with Esau. He now is able to settle in Canaan and trust that the promises of God to him and through him will go forward.

Yet it is *'by means of many tribulations that'* we enter into an experience of the kingdom of God (see Acts 14:22). Israel's special trials and testings come to him in connection with his children. In the next chapters we shall see of the difficulties he had through Dinah (ch. 34), through the birth of his last son Benjamin (ch. 35), through Joseph (ch. 37) and through Judah (ch. 38). He is confronted with a whole host of family problems which cause him great distress and drive him to move away from Shechem where he had settled (ch. 34).

1. **Pain often comes to us through those who are dearest to us**. The patriarchs were all rather irresponsible as parents. Abraham was a polygamist. Isaac showed great favouritism towards Esau. Israel had four wives and twelve sons but he was not a specially good father. We have seen how greatly he showed favouritism towards Rachel and Joseph. After his experiences with Laban in which Leah was imposed on him we can understand why he should feel this way. Yet it was not a good way to be a parent. None of the patriarchs, Abraham, Isaac and Israel, was a model parent.

Israel had **a wandering daughter**. Israel settled at Shechem. Some time later when his children were young adults, one of his daughters, Dinah, went visiting with the local Canaanites

(34:1). She was noticed by Shechem. He was an arrogant young man, the son of a prince, and forced her to have sex with him (34:2). Despite his violent ways he loved her (34:3) and urged his father to arrange for his marriage to her (34:4).

Israel himself was **a weak father**. He knew of what had happened (34:5) but he did not take any action or make any protest (34:5). Hamor was seeking to arrange a marriage when the girl's brothers arrived (34:6–7).

Then there were **two violent brothers**. Shechem's father, Hamor, proposed that the two clans intermarry and establish trade between themselves (34:8–10). Shechem was willing to pay any dowry-price that might be proposed (34:11–12).

For the moment Israel's sons pretended to go along with Hamor's suggestion, demanding only that the people of Hamor got circumcised (34:13–17). The men of the city are persuaded and they all get circumcised (34:18–24). But then, when they have just been circumcised and are immobilised with pain, Simeon and Levi kill the entire city including Hamor and Shechem (34:25–29). It is a case of sheer vindictiveness. They are avenging the assault of Dinah. It is a piece of savage reprisal. The desire for justice was taken to a barbaric extreme. Yet Israel was partly to blame. He had not taken much care of Dinah. He had done nothing when the incident first took place (34:5). If it had been Rachel's daughter he would have acted differently! Leah's daughter was being neglected by Israel, and since Israel did nothing his sons went to an extreme in slaughtering an entire community. Israel's way was weak and passive; Simeon and Levi's way was violent and extreme. The balance would have been somewhere in the middle. Israel could have protested and demanded some kind of compensation and could have made arrangements for the provision and protection of Dinah – but he did none of these things and allowed others to take vengeance into their own hands. Israel was afraid of the consequences but his protest was weak (34:30); he had taken no action so the brothers felt justified in what they had done (34:31). A weak father produced immature and violent children.

2. **Troublesome times forced Israel to realize his need of a fresh touch from God**. God takes note of times when we are in need of spiritual renewal. Israel was virtually forced to leave Shechem because of the events that had happened in connection with Dinah. Now God leads him to return to Bethel, the place where he had first met with God and he is asked to build an altar there (35:1). Israel needs to return to his original knowledge of God. Sometimes God calls us to restoration by saying to us *'do the deeds you did at first'* (Revelation 2:5).

So Israel summons his family to cleanse themselves from every hint of idolatry. They must put on a new set of clothes (speaking of a new public lifestyle) and return to the God who had delivered Israel in a day of distress (35:2–3). The entire clan travel to Bethel (35:4). God gives them special protection as they travel (35:5–6). Israel builds an altar, worships God, recalls what had happened to him many years before, and resolves that he and his family will live as worshippers and servants of the God of Abraham.

It was the end of an era. The previous generation was passing away. Deborah died (35:9). It was a hint to Israel that his father's generation was passing away and soon he would be alone as the leader of the people of God. God's people were still largely confined to the one family of Abraham; Israel would soon be its one and only leader.

God reminds Israel of his new name and new nature. He is 'Israel', someone able to be blessed by God. He is no longer 'Jacob', a manipulator and twister (35:9–10).

Then God reminds the patriarch that He Himself is 'El Shaddai'. We have come across this name before. It is the name which means 'The God who rescues the helpless'. At this time when his family are wandering into ways of sin and violence and Israel is facing danger from the Canaanites, he can know that God is 'El Shaddai', the God who comes to our aid when we need Him.

Chapter 19

Ourselves, Our God, Our Calling
(Genesis 35:10–29)

There are times when we need a reminder of who we are and where we are with God. God was reminding 'Israel' of His promises (I put it in inverted commas, '...', to make it clear that we are talking about 'Israel' the person not Israel the nation). Jacob has become 'Israel' – a fighter with God, someone who gets God's blessings by admitting defeat (35:10). God is 'El Shaddai', the God who comes to the help of the helpless.

God reminded 'Israel' of the calling that was operating in his life. 'You are going to be fruitful' said God. 'Whole nations are going to come out of you and your line of descendants' (35:11). 'The land of Canaan is going to be given to you' (35:12).

None of this was new. God had told Jacob before that his name was 'Israel' (see 32:28). God had appeared as El Shaddai – the God of the helpless – long ago in the days of Abraham. It was as the God who rescued the helpless that He came to the aid of Abraham and enabled the promises to go forward (see Genesis 17:1). And the promise of land and of prosperity had been given to 'Israel' before (see 28:13–15). So these things were not new to 'Israel'.

There are times in our lives when we need to be reminded who we are, who God is, and what our calling is. Otherwise we forget and lose our spiritual clearsightedness.

The vision of our identity, our God and our calling becomes dim and we need to be reminded all over again. God appeared to 'Israel'; it was the third time in 'Israel's' life when he had received such an experience and it came at a time when he was at his worst and needed help from God. It was a definite and powerful experience of God in visible form; then the appearance of God was withdrawn (35:13).

'Israel' responded to God's reminder. He built a stone pillar (35:14); it was his way of commemorating what had happened. He wanted to remember Bethel for ever. He poured out a drink offering (35:14); the symbolism spoke of total self-dedication in which one 'pours oneself out' to God, as Jesus poured out His soul unto death (Isaiah 53:10). He poured oil on the stone memorial (35:14); this spoke of consecration and dedication as a sacred site; in the ancient world oil was used in ceremonial consecration.

'Israel' has to trust in God's presence through many troubles. Jacob named the place 'Bethel'. He never wanted to forget the place as the place where God had twice met with him in dramatic circumstances (35:15).

Soon Jacob had difficult circumstances in which to trust God. There is **Rachel's death**. Rachel struggled in childbirth (35:16–17) and in her great distress gave her son a gloomy, pessimistic name (35:18). Jacob's sense of God's presence is still with him and he is more optimistic than Rachel. He names the new child 'Benjamin', 'son of the south' or 'son of the right hand'. Benjamin was to be regarded as the honoured son of Jacob's much-loved wife Rachel. 'Israel' built a monument to his much-loved wife and continued to travel towards Ephrah (35:19–21).

There is **Reuben's sin**. One of 'Israel's' sons sins with Bilhah, one of Jacob's concubines (35:22). It seems that as the firstborn son he wants to take from his father the leadership of the clan, and this is an ancient way of taking leadership (see 2 Samuel 16:15–23 for a similar incident).

Then there is **the passing of Isaac's generation**. Rebekah had already died. Now there were twelve sons (35:23–26) and the previous generation passes away. Isaac is the last to go. Jacob is with him at the end, and Jacob and Esau are together at his burial (35:27–29).

Jacob needed to respond to God's assurances to him

because he was in a time when everything around him was being uprooted and unsettled. Many of his sons were turning out to be disappointments to him. His wife, Rachel, was extremely precious to him. He would refer later to the day when *'Rachel died, to my sorrow'* (Genesis 48:7).

It was the end of an epoch. The main purpose of God would soon pass from Jacob to Joseph and to Judah. Reuben had disgraced himself. Simeon and Levi had proved themselves to be men of great violence. The family inheritance would pass through Judah, the fourth son. And Joseph would also have a very major part to play in the events that are about to take place.

Sometimes events happen in our lives that force us to look to the future. Jacob's ministry is not simply for his own lifetime. It is tied up with the future, with what will happen after his life has come to an end, and with the future of the kingdom of God.

The Jacob-story ends at this point. When Jacob appears again it will be in connection with the story of Joseph. The last event in the Jacob-story is that of his return to Bethel and the incidents connected with it. God gave Jacob a new revelation. We can keep going through any trouble as long as God reveals Himself to us. The troubles may be great.

The sinfulness of those close to us may be oppressive. There may be constant reminders that life is short. Our most precious companions may be taken from us. But if God appears and reminds us of who we are, who He is, and what He is promising to do – all will be well. We must not get too caught up with earthly pleasures and successes; events will soon take place that will remind us that our ultimate hope is not in this world. The question is: as life moves steadily on towards eternity are we conscious that we are laying up treasure in heaven? Do we have the conviction that we are achieving something for God? Our identity, our God, our calling are safe and that is all that really matters.

Chapter 20

The Future of Esau
(Genesis 36:1–37:1)

Before passing from the story of Jacob to the story of
Joseph, one chapter is concerned with Esau. Genesis follows
the story of a family line, but as different parts of the family-
line are left behind we are given glimpses of what happens to
the lesser lines of descent, before saying farewell to them.

So after the announcement of a new heading (36:1) we
read of Esau's sons (36:1–4) and Edom's chiefs (36:5–19),
and then of more sons of Seir (34:20–28) and more chiefs
(34:29–30). Kingship was functioning in Edom before there
was kingship in Israel (34:31–39). Genesis 34:40–43
mentions eleven districts of Edom with its eleven rulers.

Esau had a bad beginning. He was spoilt by his father and
tricked by his brother. He was strictly Isaac's firstborn son
but from the beginning it had been announced to Rebekah
that the family promises would come into being through
Jacob not through Esau. In the event Esau preferred worldly
pleasures to spiritual achievement (see 25:30). He preferred a
plate of food in the here-and-now above the ultimate
blessing of being used by God (see 25:32). He got on well
with pagan women (24:3–4) and disgraced his family
(26:34–35) by the way he lived.

Yet despite his bad beginning and despite his delayed
interest in his inheritance, it seems that he did develop a
regard for the things of God. One might guess that he came
to faith in the God of his fathers as he was going out with
four hundred men to slaughter Jacob. Jacob wrestled
with God and overcame both God and man. Esau seems to

70

have come to new attitudes as a result of Jacob's praying. Certainly by the time he met with Jacob his heart had changed (see 33:1–12). But it was too late for total spiritual recovery, and the New Testament uses the early life of Esau to warn us against persistently neglecting our inheritance so that eventually we lose it although we do not lose our position in the family of God (see Hebrews 12:16).

Although he was not the chosen channel of the line towards Israel and towards Jesus, yet God gave him many blessings that were shadows of the blessings that would come to the world through Jesus.

Esau had three major wives (36:1–3). Their names are different from those mentioned in 26:34–35 and 28:9. He probably had many wives and only three major wives are being mentioned.

Esau had five sons mentioned in 36:4–5. Esau moved into his own territory, in circumstances which are outlined in 36:6–8. The new land became known as Edom.

Esau had thirteen grandsons mentioned in 36:9–14. Fourteen of Esau's descendants became chiefs of clans. They are mentioned in 35:15–19. There were sons and grandsons of Seir also living in the same land of Edom, mentioned in 36:20–28; one of them was famous for discovering hot springs in the wilderness (36:24). Seven chiefs came from these people (36:29–30). The Edomites had kings before there were any kings in Israel. Eight of them are mentioned in 36:31–39.

Eleven Edomite chiefs ruled eleven districts of Edom.

What is the point of all of this detail given to us concerning Esau and his descendants?

1. It was an indication that **even the non-elect Esau could be blessed by God**. The choice of Jacob as God's channel for the line leading toward Jesus did not mean that Esau was rejected from every blessing altogether. We need to know that in the church of Jesus there are vessels chosen for honour. But among the saved even those not chosen to be famous or for special ministry can be blessed by God as well!

2. It was an indication that **God's blessings for those who are not chosen for special purposes can be quite similar to those for God's special channels of blessing**. Jacob was promised a seed; Esau had a seed as well. Jacob was promised land; Esau had land as well. Jacob was given the promise that kings would come from him; Esau had kings as well.

3. **God's chosen instruments go through a tougher time but their blessings are given at a higher level**. Esau had a seed as well as Jacob but that seed did not lead to Jesus. Esau had land as well as Jacob but that land would not lead to the new heavens and new earth. Actually for a long time Jacob's people lost the land and were taken to Egypt. The promised land for them would be the whole glorified earth given to all believers through Jesus. The promise is like the one given to Esau but is fulfilled at a higher level. Esau had kings as well as Jacob and they were given to him before they were given to Israel, but that line of kings did not lead to Jesus.

Those who are rejected by God for special use may have all of the earthly blessings that God's special instruments have, but eventually God uses His special instruments at a higher level.

It ought to let us know that when others seem to be doing better than we are, at an earthly level, our inheritance will come to us more slowly but it will be altogether greater. Esau got plenty of present blessings but the Edomites that were his descendants would have a tough time in the future. They would have hostile attitudes (see Numbers 20:21). The Amalekites and Edomites were descended from Esau but would not experience the blessings of Jesus. Only through faith in Jesus is the history of Esau reversed. Any remaining descendants of Esau, whoever they might be, can find salvation in a son of Jacob, our Lord Jesus Christ. Esau had his own blessings but they were nothing compared to what would come to Jacob, God's chosen vessel living in the land of Canaan (37:1).

Chapter 21

A Young Man and His Destiny
(Genesis 37:2–36)

The story of Genesis now turns mainly to Joseph, although Jacob will come into the story later. As with all of the patriarchs, Abraham, Isaac, Jacob, Joseph – Joseph is a person with a special destiny in the plans and purposes of God.

1. **Joseph is a man with a calling** (Genesis 37:2–11). His background was a fairly ordinary one. He was a shepherd (37:2). Like many young men he had his own problems. He was a tale-bearer towards his brothers (37:2). The fact that Jacob made a favourite out of him caused a great deal of pride in the young Joseph and a great deal of bitterness and jealousy in his brothers (37:3–4). The important thing about him is that he had a destiny in the purpose of God. At this point in the story we do not know what that destiny is but like all believers in the promises of God, he has a spiritual gift. His gift is an unusual one: he is able to receive dreams from God which give accurate predictions of the future (37:5). At this point in his life the dreams are about himself. They come more than once (37:6–8, 9).

Joseph makes the mistake of sharing his dreams with his family. This does not do him any good. His brothers do not think well of him for his sharing his visions about himself. It only creates pride in the young Joseph and jealousy in his brothers (37:10–11). Even Jacob rebukes him, although he is thoughtful about the matter since he had received his own greatest spiritual experiences in two dreams, one at Bethel and another at Peniel.

Every Christian has a calling, something in which God will give him or her a little eminence in the kingdom of our Lord Jesus Christ.

2. **Joseph needed training** (Genesis 37:12–35). As with every man and woman that God uses. Joseph needs some preparation. God has chosen him. He has a destiny and a spiritual gift, but God also wants to work in Joseph Himself.

His training starts **suddenly**. There is a day in his life which starts as a fairly ordinary day. His brothers are working as shepherds. Joseph, as his father's favourite, is at home (37:12). Jacob sends him on a journey of about 80 kilometres to enquire about the welfare of his brothers (37:13–14).

His training starts **surprisingly**. Jacob did not feel that Joseph would be in any danger, but something unexpected happened. The brothers were not easily to be found. However Joseph persevered in his search for them and discovered that they had moved a further twenty-five kilometres away to Dothan (37:15–17). Shechem was a regular visiting-place for Abraham's family but Dothan was further away from where they were known. The brothers were evidently camping at a spot where they felt they could do as they liked and no one would know what they were doing. They see Joseph coming and because they were far from home immediately see an opportunity to get rid of Joseph once and for ever. With the exception of Reuben they all wish to kill him (37:18–20). What they hate most about him is the feeling they have that his dreams might come true. They are hoping to overthrow his predictions. *'We shall see what will become of his dreams,'* they say (37:20).

Reuben persuades them not to kill him there and then but to allow him to die of exposure in one of the many deep pits of the area (37:21–22). Secretly he plans to rescue Joseph. They proceed to carry out their plans (37:23–24) but again the unexpected happens. At a time when Reuben was not present a caravan of Ishmaelite traders pass by (also called Midianites and Medanites in 37:28, 36). They are on their way to Egypt with goods for sale (37:25). The brothers see a way of making some money and getting rid of Joseph at the same time. They sell Joseph as a slave (37:26–28). Reuben comes back, finds out what has happened but it is too late to rescue Joseph (37:29–30). He has no choice but to go along with the brothers' plan. They convince Jacob that Joseph has been accidentally killed by a wild animal (37:31–35).

The important point of the story is that the events are surprising and obviously are being controlled by God. If Jacob had not sent Joseph on that day, if the brothers had not been a bit further away from home, if the traders had not been coming by, if Reuben had not been away at the time . . . . The precise set of circumstances were all necessary for this unexpected event to happen. But God was in control and the chosen time for God to set some events in motion had arrived. God sets events in motion that prepare to train us, prepare for our future, prepare the way for His kingdom. They can be sudden and surprising. When we look back on them we see clearly that God was in what happened. The circumstances are so surprising. God is behind what is happening.

So it will happen in the life of every Christian. The greater God's plans for us, the greater will be His training. Joseph is a gifted young man but he needs more than one kind of training before he will be ready for his life's work. A shepherd cannot become a senior administrator in the service of Pharaoh, king of Egypt, without some preparation, some training in character, and some unexpected manipulations of God. But this is what is happening to Joseph. It is painful but purposeful. God knows what He is doing. The last line of this part of the story is a hint that greater things are in store for Joseph. *'The Midianites had sold him to Potiphar, an officer of Pharaoh'* (37:36).

Chapter 22

The Story of Judah
(Genesis 38:1–30)

The change in the story from Joseph to Judah might seem rather surprising. Yet there is a reason why we need to know a little of Judah, as will appear later.

The story is as follows. Judah marries a Canaanite and has three sons (38:1–5). Later the oldest of his half-Canaanite sons married and Judah had a daughter-in-law, Tamar. When Tamar was unexpectedly widowed it was the custom that a brother in the family would see that a son was born to her, so that her part of the family would continue (38:6–8). The second son wanted the pleasure of spending the night with Tamar but did not want to see a son born to her (38:9–10). 'Levirate marriage' had its problems (and still does in parts of the world today) but it was a way of providing a son for a widow. God was displeased that a widow should be treated in the way Tamar was treated; the second son died.

At this point Judah, the father-in-law, decides to shrug off this kind of responsibility for Tamar (38:11). Although he pretends that his third son might one day provide for her, Judah plans to do nothing about her plight as a widow without a son to protect her.

Some time later Judah himself loses his partner. Judah was evidently known to be the kind of person who would make use of an easily available girl. Tamar decides to exploit his vulnerability (38:12–15) and at the same time makes sure that she has proof of his identity (38:16–19). Judah was not able to reclaim his pledge to the girl (38:20–23) and the matter was dropped. But three months later when Tamar was found to be pregnant the truth came out (38:24–26). Later still Tamar had twins (38:27). One of the twins, although not born first, put out a hand first and received a scarlet thread which marked his doing so (38:28–30). Once again, *'the elder served the younger,'* for it was the one who put out a hand first who was the ancestor of Jesus (see Ruth 4:18; Matthew 1:3; Luke 3:33).

What is the point and place of this story in the book of Genesis?

1. **It underlines that God's plans for Israel are entirely from His graciousness**. Again and again in the story of the family of Abraham we discover that the 'heroes' of the story are sinners like everyone else on planet earth. Abraham was a man who could lie out of fear. Isaac could be deceived by his appetite for a good meal. Jacob was notorious as a crook and deceiver. Now here are the twelve brothers who will become the forefathers of the twelve tribes of Israel. But it has to be said that God's history of salvation is not making use of people who are specially godly. Here are the twelve ancestors of Israel. They are happy to see Joseph killed although he is one of the brothers. One of these brothers – Judah – is exceptionally callous. It all makes it perfectly plain that God's plans go forward by His taking sinners and using them without being put off by their wickedness and brutality.

2. **The story explains the great change that came into Judah's life**. It seems that this event brought about a great change in Judah. At the time of this incident, he was a man with a well-known tendency to immorality and with a harsh, uncompassionate spirit, a man who cared nothing for his brother Joseph or his daughter-in-law Tamar. When she was found to be unexpectedly pregnant he had only one thing to say: *'Let her be burned'* (38:4). It was Judah who made the suggestion about selling Joseph to the Ishmaelites. *'What profit is it to us if we kill our brother?'* he had said. *'Let us sell him to the Ishmaelites...'* (37:26–27). Judah was at that stage a cruel, callous, womanizing brute.

Yet a little while later we find Judah pleading for mercy for his father (44:18–34). He became like Jesus in being willing to offer himself as a substitute who would suffer in the place of his brother (44:33) and was himself distressed at the thought of more pain and suffering coming upon the elderly Jacob (44:34). It was this plea that brought Joseph to the point of breaking down in distress (45:1). What caused this amazing change of character in Judah? It has to be the event that took place here in Genesis 38.

3. **The story of Judah leads to the choice of Judah as the tribe of the Son of David**. Later on in the book when we come to the predictive outline of what will happen to the sons of Judah, we shall find it is Judah who is chosen to be the royal line. Although all the tribes of Judah came into being by God's grace, yet there was a certain amount of appropriateness in how God used them in days to come. Reuben forfeited blessing because of his immorality (49:4), Simon and Levi were notorious for their violence (49:5–7). It was the fourth son, Judah, who was given the promise of sovereignty and kingship (49:8–12). Although God's grace is so amazing it is not necessary to explain why He should give privileges to anyone, yet it is also true that God likes to give rewards and that special privileges come to those who please God. What pleased God is that a savage man became a compassionate man. And what turned Judah into a man of sensitivity and compassion was the disgrace and shame that came upon him at this time of his life. It is an encouragement to all who have badly fallen. What could be the greatest disgrace of our lives might after all have a place in the story of the kingdom of God. When God chose to send Jesus through one of the tribes of Israel, He did not choose the tribe of the favourite, Joseph. He chose the tribe of Judah! God was pleased with a sinner who became a saint. Judah the profligate became Judah the compassionate.

Chapter 23

Preparation for Ministry

(Genesis 39:1–23)

Joseph was being trained. His cushy, easy life as his father's favourite had come to an abrupt end and now he was a slave in the household of Potiphar. It was painful but it was all part of God's training for Joseph.

1. **God's training involved a mixture of pain and comfort**. When God is training us, for a while we feel that God is against us. 'Why is this happening to me?' we say. But then it becomes clear to us that God is still with us. God knows how to mix troubles and comforts. Joseph is a slave. He was owned by Potiphar (39:1). His comfortable life is lost for ever. But God was with him (39:2). It was obvious to Potiphar that he had acquired an unusual man (39:3) and soon he gave over the running of the household to Joseph (39:4). When Potiphar prospered more than ever (39:5), he gave Joseph full control of almost everything in the household (39:6a).

Joseph's experience was a mixture. Initially it must have been a very embittering situation. He must have felt sharply the injustice of his brothers' wickedness. God seemed to have betrayed him. In his dreams his brothers had been bowing down to him but they were not bowing down just yet.

Yet mixed in with the sufferings there was a certain amount of satisfaction. Joseph was clearly a capable administrator and the strange workings of God were giving him rich experience.

2. **Joseph's integrity was tested**. He was handsome (39:6b). Potiphar's wife begins to give sexual invitations to Joseph

(39:7). He refuses. It would be ingratitude towards Potiphar (39:8–9a); it would be taking the one thing Potiphar has withheld (39:9b); it would be sin against God (39:9c).

The temptation must have been severe. He was a young man with the normal temptations of young men. He was a long way from home. The temptation was persistent (39:10). One day Potiphar's wife was exceptionally insistent (39:11–12a). But throughout the entire situation Joseph was a model in his resisting temptation. He said 'no' (39:8); he gave clear reasons why he was saying 'no' (39:8–9). He remained firm despite constant pressure (39:10). He would not put himself in a situation where temptation was close (*'he did not listen'* nor would he *'be with her'*). Finally he ran far from her when she was insistent (39:11–13).

3. **He was tested by extreme injustice**. One might think that after his withstanding temptation God would reward Joseph, but the conflict did not get better; it got worse. Being rejected by Joseph brings about extreme hatred. First she wants him; them she hates him. She calls in the men of the house (39:14) and blames her husband. In doing so she reveals that she does not have a good relationship with her husband (39:15). No wonder she has been looking to Joseph for pleasure. She puts forward her own deceitful version of what has happened (39:16–19) slandering Joseph and portraying him in the worst possible light. It all shows she had no love for him, despite her invitations.

Joseph must have felt greatly the ill-treatment he was getting. He had shown great faithfulness towards God and toward his master. But all the reward he gets is slander. He is quite unable to defend himself. The evidence points against him. The woman has his cloak in her hands. He has no way of proving his version of what has happened. It is quite impossible for him to defend himself.

In a strange way this too is part of Joseph's training. Anyone who is going to be used by God is not going to get praise from the world, and he or she is likely to get a lot of false rumours and false stories. Early in one's life one needs to get used to withstanding slander. There is nothing Joseph can do.

Potiphar's wife tells her version of the story, and Potiphar is furious (39:19). Perhaps however he did not altogether believe his wife's story because Joseph was not put to death, as could easily have happened. Instead he is put into the private dungeon of Pharaoh and his officials (39:20).

God knows how to mix troubles and comforts. It is God's plan to allow troubles to come upon His people. We do not like sufferings and testings but we need them. *'We ... rejoice in tribulations, knowing that tribulation brings about persever-ance ...'* (Romans 5:3). It is necessary for us to be trained and humbled and driven to rely on God. But at the same time God knows how to limit our troubles so that they do not entirely crush us. Just as God had given favour in the house of Potiphar, God now gave him favour in the prison of Pharaoh (39:21). And what happened in Potiphar's house also happened in Pharaoh's prison. Joseph soon became the chief administrator of the entire prison. Handling prisoners was a more difficult matter than handling the possessions of Potiphar. It was the same area of training; Joseph was an administrator. But the level of training was now higher. God was preparing Joseph for the day when he would be administering the entire land of Egypt (41:41).

God was training Joseph for ministry. Every Christian has a ministry and we can expect God to supervise our lives so that we get training for what God is planning to do through us. It will often involve painful situations. Yet in the situations He puts us in, we shall find that we get practise in what He intends to give us as our calling in life. The greater the calling, the greater the training.

Chapter 24

Developing a Gift
(Genesis 40:1–41:13)

From his teenage years Joseph knew that he had a gift. He
was able to receive and to interpret dreams. He knew that his
'gift of dreams' was to be used in the kingdom of God. He
had known that his parents and his brothers would be junior
to him in some way. His dreams when he was back in Canaan
had let him know that he was to be an eminent person of
some kind.

God gave Joseph time to adjust to his new life. When God
gives us a firm shove in the direction of a new life, we often
find it painful. For a long time we dream of going back.
Maybe we pray night and day that God will take us back to
where we were. If Joseph believed in prayer – as he surely did
– he must have prayed day and night that God would take
him back to Canaan.

Joseph was 17 years old when we first met him (37:2). He
was thirty years old when he became Pharaoh's senior
administrator (see 41:46). The total time when he was in
Potiphar's house and Pharaoh's prison must have been
about twelve years. Maybe – at a guess – he spent six years
in Potiphar's house and six years in Pharaoh's dungeon.

The gift of God gets exercised. Joseph had been in prison
for some years when two newcomers were added to the
number of prisoners. Pharaoh's cupbearer and Pharaoh's
baker both offended him and found themselves in prison
(40:1–4). Both of them had dreams and Joseph finds out
(40:5–8a). Joseph has a gift of interpreting dreams. He

82

instantly knows he will be able to interpret both dreams. *'Do not interpretations belong to God?'* he asks (40:8b).

Joseph has been in troubles and tribulations for some years but during those years his gift has not disappeared. He has never lost the gift of dreams which he had when he was seventeen years old. Now he gets an opportunity to use the gift that God gave him. It is not that he is going to be famous or highly appreciated. He is only an administrator in a dungeon. But it gives him the opportunity to know that the ability which God had given him has not been lost or withdrawn.

He has an assurance about his gift. He is quite certain that he will be able to interpret these dreams. A man or a woman with a gift knows about it! A preacher knows he can preach. Singers know they can sing. People with gifts of healing often know that when they pray healings are likely to take place. The gifts of God 'manifest' themselves. Each supernatural ability is a 'manifestation' of the Holy Spirit (1 Corinthians 12:7). We sometimes ask 'How can I know my gift?' It is not a question that should trouble us too much. A gift of God shows itself. The only difficulty is that the gifted person may think that everyone should be doing what he or she is doing. A preacher thinks everyone ought to be able to preach! A person with the gift of hospitality thinks that everyone should have his or her ability. A gift comes very naturally to its possessor. Joseph knows he will be able to interpret this dream. Soon he gives a happy interpretation of the cupbearer's dream (40:9–13).

The manipulations of God are irresistible. When God is working powerfully in our lives to train us, to chasten us, to put us where He wants us, His manipulations are quite irresistible. We may try to change or alter what God is doing but we shall find it quite impossible to stop the progress of events. When God puts us into a tight spot we shall discover that all of our attempts to extricate ourselves will fail. Joseph knows the cupbearer will be released, so he takes the opportunity to try to get himself out of prison (40:14). He tries to get someone to take notice of his troubles (*'Keep me* *in mind when it goes well with you . . . '*). He tries to get through to the highest authority (*'Do me a kindness by mentioning me to Pharaoh'*). He tries to get sympathy (*'I was kidnapped . . . '*). And he tries to assert his innocence (*'I have done nothing that they should have put me into this dungeon . . . '*). But none of this is going to succeed. God will not allow Joseph to extricate himself from the powerful training that God is giving to him. God's plans are moving forward irresistibly and exactly on time.

The cupbearer soon has further evidence of Joseph's gift. For Joseph gives a sad interpretation of the baker's dream (40:16–19) and soon both interpretations are fulfilled. The cupbearer is restored and the baker is executed (40:20–22). But none of his attempts to get attention succeed. God is moving irresistibly and Joseph's struggles to get himself released before God's time simply fail. The cupbearer forgot him (40:23). Joseph remained in prison for another two years (41:1).

'Salvation is from the LORD' (as Jonah put it; see Jonah 3:9). When God is moulding our character and preparing for our future, He acts in a most amazing and powerful way. He can move people around with the greatest of ease but when we try to get ourselves out of the tough discipline that God has imposed upon us we find we simply cannot get the situation to change. It moves along steadily under the mighty control of God and there is nothing we can do to stop the progress of events. Our release from God's discipline has to come from Him. Until He acts we shall remain in confinement under His mighty preparation.

The gift gets noticed. A gift 'manifests' itself. We do not have to say a word about it. If what we think is a gift from God really is a gift it will get noticed. Pharaoh has a dream (41:1–7); no one can interpret it (41:8). But then the cupbearer remembers Joseph (41:9–13). The ability of Joseph was perfectly obvious to the cupbearer. Joseph did not have to persuade the cupbearer that he had the gift of interpreting dreams. The ability simply showed itself in a way that was perfectly plain and obvious. This is what a gift is like. You do not have to persuade people about it. It will speak for itself.

Chapter 25

Hearing From God

(Genesis 41:14–36)

Pharaoh had received a revelation from God yet he did not understand the revelation he had received.

Joseph's period of suffering and training ended as abruptly as it had begun. Just as the chastening of God may start very abruptly, so the end comes very abruptly. Many years before Joseph had been abruptly plunged into suffering when he left his father's house one day not realising that he would never return to it until after his father's death. Similarly the end comes suddenly. Joseph is in the dungeon. He has not had any hope of escape for over two years. For a long time there has been nothing he can do except pray. He is longing to escape but it seems that release is never going to come.

Suddenly *'Pharaoh sent for Joseph and they brought him **quickly** out of the dungeon'* (41:14). There came a knock at the door. 'Joseph! Get shaved Here are some new clothes. Hurry! Pharaoh wants to see you!'

Pharaoh is given a word from God through Joseph. We can learn much from these events about how God speaks to us.

1. **God uses Joseph in revealing His will when he has learned humility**. Joseph has lost the arrogance of his younger years. Pharaoh says to him *'I hear you are able to interpret dreams'* (41:15). Joseph's answer is *'It is not in me. God will give Pharaoh a favourable answer'* (41:16). One cannot imagine Joseph answering this way when he was a teenager. As a seventeen-year-old teenager he had been proud of his gift and ready to boast about what he knew. But now all of that

has gone. Joseph has been forced over many years to acknowledge that everything about him is subject to the kingship of God. His life, his gifts, what is going to happen to him – everything is in the hands of God. He now speaks with simple but honest humility. 'It is not me; it is God'. He is ready to be used as a channel of revelation to Pharaoh.

2. **God may speak in stages**. It was that way with Pharaoh. He first received a dream, but he needed more. God wanted him to hunt out the significance of what God was saying to him. Pharaoh tells the dream. He was by the Nile and saw first seven fat cows and then seven starved cows (41:17–21). Then in a second dream he saw seven full 'ears' of corn followed by seven poor 'ears' where the corn had been blighted by the hot east wind blowing in from the desert (41:22–24a). Pharaoh had told the dream to his pagan magicians but they could not explain the dream (41:24b).

After the dream he still feels the need of explanation. God is speaking to him in stages and he does not yet see what God is saying. It is this that leads to his sending for Joseph.

3. **The revelation from God finally comes with clarity and conviction**. Joseph is quite confident and speaks with authority and clarity. When someone has a gift or has received a true revelation from God, there is always assurance concerning the gift. It is known with confidence by the person who has the gift and it is recognized by the person for whom the gift is intended.

Joseph knows the two dreams make the same point (41:25). It is God who orders the affairs of nature, and He is about to act (41:26). There will be seven years of abundance followed by seven years of famine (41:27–31). The fact that the revelation is given twice over means that the events are about to happen speedily (41:32).

4. **God's revelations are given with practical purpose**. Joseph does more than interpret the dream. He gives detailed instructions as to what should be done. A gifted administrator should be appointed (41:33). He must be gifted and wise since it will take some skill in management and administration. He must be able to arrange a whole nation's

agricultural affairs during a time of plenty and then during a time of need. It will take a gifted man to cope with the change that takes place after the first seven years. And it will take a gifted man to handle the threat of suffering that will come during the second seven years. The administrator must be accountable to Pharaoh himself and must be someone Pharaoh can trust (41:34). The administrator must not be corrupt. He must take a twenty per cent tax of the corn which is grown during the prosperous years (41:35). The grain must be stored and it will give ample supplies for the years of leanness that follow (41:36).

God's word is like this; it is highly practical. The modern Christian needs to hear from God. The revelation Joseph received and which Joseph passed on was not a piece of writing. It might be asked, 'Now that we have the Bible do we need living revelations like this?' To which it must be said: the Bible must not be read as a **cold** revelation. It must be received as living oracles of God. We must hear God in His word with the same kind of immediacy and consciousness of Him as Joseph had when God was illuminating his mind to understand Pharaoh's dream. When Pharaoh had his dream before him he still needed further clarification. Reading God's word is similar. When we have the written word in our hands we need a 'Joseph'; we need an interpreter. The interpreter might be another person as on the occasion when the Ethiopian eunuch of Acts 8:31 wanted someone to guide him. But finally the 'Joseph', the 'interpreter' has to be the Holy Spirit.

Chapter 26

Full Conviction
(Genesis 41:37–57)

5. **God's word was widely recognized**. It is wonderful when God speaks with indisputable power and authority. Pharaoh recognized instantly that what Joseph had said was from God. *'The thing was good in the eyes of Pharaoh and in the eyes of all his servants'* (41:37; the translation, 'it seemed good', is misleading; it **was** good). Pharaoh also recognizes that there is some kind of *'Spirit of God'* in Joseph (41:38).

When the word of God comes with power it proves itself. It carries its own convicting power. When God's Spirit is powerfully at work, no one has to talk about 'proving' that something is a word from God. The word comes with such power that it proves itself! Paul said his gospel came *'with full conviction'* (1 Thessalonians 1:5). It might be asked: who had the 'conviction' Paul or his hearers? The answer is: both! When God's word comes with power the speaker is fully assured he is speaking from God, and the hearers are also fully convinced they are hearing from God.

6. **The channel of God's word came into a position of eminence and importance**. After years of suffering Joseph was able to be exalted without becoming too proud. Our spiritual giftedness makes itself known. Where the church is functioning as it should giftedness will be recognized. Every Christian has at least one gift of the Holy Spirit; every Christian has some ministry within the church of Jesus Christ. Our gift leads us into our right place in the functioning of God's church. It is a wonderful thing when we get to be where we ought to be and where God has destined us. It

89

does not need any kind of manipulation. Joseph's efforts to get himself out of Pharaoh's dungeon had not worked at all. When at last he was ready it took no manipulation at all. With the greatest of ease and without his doing anything at all he was lifted into the position that he had been trained for. Pharaoh recognized that God had revealed the future to Joseph (41:39); he recognized his suitability as the administrator that Egypt needed (41:39) and immediately gave him great authority (41:40–41). He was given the sign of authority, the signet ring (41:42). He was given clothing that gave him dignity, and a gold necklace that was the sign of his importance. When God had started his painful training many years before he had lost importance and at the same time he lost the coat with long sleeves. Now he was given back importance and the clothing that went with it.

He now had freedom to act with authority (41:43). (There is a difficult word in the original that seems to be an Egyptian word meaning 'Bow the knee!'). All authority was put into his hand and nothing happened except through him. This is like the present position of Jesus. Jesus is the king of the universe and everything that the Father does He does through the rule of His Son. When God exalts us we share in this sovereignty of Jesus, and to a lesser and limited extent we reign and rule with Jesus. It is not a matter of worldly triumph. It is a matter of ruling in a kingdom of love and compassion. Joseph ruled Egypt in order to be a blessing to Egypt and to be like a father and a shepherd over the people.

Joseph was given an Egyptian name to make him acceptable to the people (41:45). His marriage to an Egyptian priest's daughter must also have brought him some acceptance (41:45). He was given work to do which took him through the length and breadth of the land of Egypt (41:45b–46).

7. **God's word through Joseph had prediction in it and the fulfilment confirmed that it was truly from God**. If there had not been seven years of plenty followed by seven years of famine, Joseph's word from God would have been suspect.

When there is prediction in God's word, fulfilment is a vital matter. As Joseph had said, there were seven years of plenty and Joseph followed the word that he had revealed from God (41:47–49).

God keeps His word. Whether it is some small revelation God has given to us about our future or whether it is some great prediction that comes in the Scriptures, God will keep His word. During this time Joseph had two sons, Manasseh ('He who causes forgetfulness') his firstborn, and Ephraim ('Fruitfulness') his second son. God has repaid Joseph for his many years of trouble with great happiness and fruitfulness (41:50–52).

The seven years of famine followed, also confirming the authenticity of God's word (41:53–57).

8. **Faithfulness to God's word brings Joseph many rewards**. Joseph had been utterly frank and straightforward with Pharaoh. He had been as faithful in telling Pharaoh about famine as he had been about telling Pharaoh's baker about death. His faithfulness is rewarded. He has position, authority, a family, joy which makes him forget all his sorrows, fruitfulness which gives him a sense of fulfilment and satisfaction. The famine was severe throughout the world. The events that have happened are about to bring Joseph into contact with Canaan. His calling involves the nations of the world. At this time Joseph had given up any expectation of ever seeing Jacob or his brothers again. His new life made him forget 'all his father's house' (41:51). But part of his reward was involvement in the plan of God for the line of Jacob. Joseph was probably wondering whether he had finished for ever with Jacob and his ten cruel brothers. He had many years before announced God's word to his brothers when he told them that he would rule over them. At that time he revealed God's word with great immaturity and foolishness. But God's word stands firm. The story is moving towards the time when the fulfilment of God's word in the minutest detail is about to take place. Joseph is faithful to God's word. When the word is vindicated, he will be vindicated as well.

Chapter 27

Bringing Others to Repentance
(Genesis 42:1–21)

Joseph was perhaps wondering whether he would ever see Jacob or his brothers again. His new life made him forget *'all his father's house'* (41:51). God deals powerfully and sovereignly with His people. He had trained and led Joseph for many years. Now the story turns to the way in which Jacob and the brothers of Joseph were confronted with their past. They were a weak and fallible people. Jacob had in days gone by been crafty and selfish. This weakness in his life had largely been dealt with by God. But he still is prone to these sins.

The children of Jacob are also full of weaknesses. We have seen Dinah's foolishness, and the violence of Jacob's sons. We have seen the immorality of Reuben and the brothers' jealousy of Joseph and Benjamin.

Jacob and his family felt the effects of the drought in Canaan and soon Joseph's brothers come to Egypt in search of food (42:1–3). Just as God had used troubles in Joseph's life, so He was now using distresses in the life of Jacob's family. Jacob was unwilling to send Benjamin because he was making a favourite of Benjamin just as he had once made a favourite of Joseph (42:4). The ten brothers arrived and were presented to Joseph. They bowed down before him – and so fulfilled the dream that Joseph had had over twenty years before (42:5–6). It must have been a deeply moving day when Joseph recognized them (42:7).

How should Joseph treat them? He could have treated them with **revenge**. He had the power and the opportunity to put them into a dungeon for ten years just as he had been enslaved and imprisoned for many years. He could have **gloated**, lording it over them, ridiculing them, making them feel guilty. He did none of those things.

1. **He treated them with restraint**. He was not in a hurry to say who he was. He wanted to help them but helping others often involves a sense of timing. One has to wait until the time is right in helping them. There is no value in 'casting one's pearls before swine' (see Matthew 7:6). So at first Joseph does not reveal himself but treats them as foreigners and acts roughly towards them (42:7). It is not the way he feels but it is the way he acts. He knows them but they do not know him (42:8). God is often the same in His treatment of us. For His own reasons God often seems to treat us with roughness but it is not the way He feels. The rough treatment we get is for His own purposes but we can be sure He has a heart of love.

2. **He wants them to face themselves and their own story**. He treats them roughly until they start to give an account of themselves. He knows that God has a purpose for the whole family of Jacob, and remembers the revelations he had about them many years previously (42:9). He falsely accuses them (42:9). He had experienced false accusation from Potiphar's wife. Now they experience false accusation from him. They begin to tell their story. They have come to get food (42:10). They are twelve brothers, they say (42:11). Twenty years have gone by since they got rid of Joseph but they still have him on their minds. They do not speak of eleven brothers but of twelve! They have not forgotten what they did to Joseph. When you do something wicked you might keep it secret for twenty years but it will still haunt you. You are not able to forget it; the guilt of it stays with you for decades. Under further pressure they mention Benjamin and Joseph (42:12–14). So Joseph now knows that Benjamin is alive. They have not got rid of Benjamin as they had got rid of him. After their wickedness towards him they had been restrained from going any further. He continues to accuse them and gets them to search their hearts. He now wants to

find out their attitude towards Benjamin and threatens them with imprisonment until Benjamin is brought to him (42:15–16). He puts them in prison (42:18). They had sold him into captivity; now he lets them experience captivity. He keeps them together. He is wanting to bring his entire family to repentance. He wants each man to admit his guilt not only to himself but also to one another. Then he makes some suggestions which will test their attitudes to each other (42:19–20). How will they feel if one of them suffers but the others are released? That is what happened to Joseph himself. One of the twelve – Joseph – had suffered but the others had an easier time. He wants them to think about that. How will they feel if he demands to see Benjamin? Benjamin, Rachel's second son, is now Jacob's favourite, a replacement for Joseph. Will they want to get rid of him? Will they be glad to have Benjamin in prison while they escape?

At last he brings them to admit their guilt. *'Truly we are guilty,'* they say (42:21) They admit it to each other (*'They said each man to his brother . . . '*). They admit their terrible lack of compassion. (*'We saw his distress . . . we would not listen . . . '*).

They admit their sense of being under God's judgement (*'Therefore this distress has come upon us'*).

God works in our lives to bring us to honesty and to repentance. It generally takes a certain amount of pressure before we will truly admit that we are the way we are. When we start telling the truth to ourselves, God is ready to bless us.

Chapter 28

Under Pressure From God

(Genesis 42:22–43:14)

Joseph's brothers have come a long way in a short space of time. For twenty years they have refused to admit to themselves or to any one else what they did to Joseph. Now they are admitting it to their own hearts and to one another. Reuben reminds them of how they had refused to listen to a word of restraint (42:22). They know they are being brought to face themselves in a day of 'reckoning' (42:22).

Joseph is not enjoying any of this! **It is exactly parallel to what happens whenever God allows us to suffer**. It is not because He is powerless. And it is not because He is cruel. He knows about what is happening. He could stop it but He does not. He does not enjoy our sufferings. But He knows about them and allows them to continue for the moment for His own purposes. Joseph has his own purposes to bring repentance and restoration and provision for his entire family. He has to do what he is doing. But he is not enjoying it. He goes out and weeps with grief and emotion at what is happening to his brothers (42:23–24a).

He goes back and carries on doing what he has to do. He takes one of them, Simeon, and lets them see him being bound (42:24b). **It gives them a sample of the kind of thing they did to Joseph**. They are sent away with food and with their money returned to them (42:25) and they leave (42:26).

Then as they are travelling back they discover the returned money (42:27). They are utterly dismayed. Their very lives depend on the food they hope to get from Joseph and yet

God seems to be blocking any hope of Joseph's having any goodwill towards them (42:28). Everything seems to be working against them. **It is the same experience that Joseph had.** Joseph could have said 'If only my father had not sent me to find my brothers, if only they had not moved away to Dothan, if only Reuben had not been absent when the Ishmaelite traders came by . . .'. God seemed to be working against Joseph. Now God seems to be working against the brothers, and there is nothing they can do about it.

Then they get back home and tell the whole story to Jacob (42:29–34). And just as it had brought back the past to the ten brothers so it brings back the past to Jacob. What will Jacob do? Will he continue to show favouritism to Benjamin as he did to Joseph? As they unpack their sacks they discover all their money has been returned (42:35). They have got all of their grain without paying anything! It seems as if they are thieves, and they will be unable to defend themselves. **Again, it is a repetition of the experience of Joseph.** Joseph had been accused by Potiphar's wife and had been unable to defend himself.

It leads to accusation and blame. Jacob says *'You have taken two of my children and now you want to take Benjamin!'* (42:36). Reuben makes a generous offer (42:37); it is the first sign of willingness to make sacrifices for the sake of someone else. For the first time one of the brothers is willing to act with kindness and concern for Jacob. It is the first indication of distress at what has happened and a willingness to make amends. **Joseph is having some success in bringing his brothers to repentance.**

But Jacob has not come to the point of abandoning his discrimination in favour of the children of Rachel. He will let Simeon perish rather than release Benjamin (42:38). However God knows how to increase the pressure on us and drive us into a corner. The famine continues (43:1) and Jacob and his family are soon at the end of their resources again. **Joseph is acting in faith and patience.** He expects the famine to continue and believes that the sheer pressure of circumstances will bring his brothers back to him again.

Soon the food in Jacob's family has come to an end (43:2) and Jacob wants them to go back to Egypt. He is desperate in wanting to hold on to Benjamin but Judah points out that there will be no help from Egypt unless Benjamin goes with them (43:3–5).

Jacob is in a fix. He loves Benjamin with a love that is almost idolatrous. All his life he had loved Rachel very deeply and her two children Joseph and Benjamin. Now Benjamin was the last of the three that were left to him. He was exceedingly precious to Jacob. **He is being asked to trust the most precious thing he has to God**.

It again leads to accusation and blame. This time Jacob criticizes them for telling the truth (43:6). They try to defend themselves before him (43:7). It is the same atmosphere of criticism and mutual accusation that was present years ago, when the brothers were jealous of Joseph.

Yet there are signs that the brothers are coming to a new love and graciousness towards each other. Jacob is not willing to surrender Benjamin but now Judah offers to take responsibility for Benjamin (43:8–9). While they are arguing they are delaying (43:10) and the food supplies are running out.

Jacob has to give in (43:11–14). **Once again he is forced to a high level of trust and dependence on God**. *'If this is the way it must be . . . . '* He has no choice. *'May El Shaddai grant you compassion'*; it is the name for God which has the sense 'The God who is Almighty to rescue' and is used in desperate situations (see Genesis 17:1; 28:3; 35:11). *'If I am bereaved, I am bereaved,'* says Jacob.

Joseph is taking the time and trouble to bring his entire family to face themselves. Jacob must come to terms with his favouritism and discrimination. The brothers must ask themselves whether they are to continue covering up their sin and treating their father and each other with cruelty and selfishness.

Chapter 29

Love Must Be Tough

(Genesis 43:15–34)

Joseph is having some success. His treatment of his family is slowly bringing them to repentance. The brothers return to Egypt with double the money they need and with Benjamin (43:15). Joseph is delighted to see Benjamin. Not only is he glad to see his brother; it is also a sign that his brothers have not treated Benjamin in the way that they treated him. It is a sign that Jacob has been willing to put his trust in God above his favouritism towards Benjamin. He immediately arranges a party to celebrate and feast with his brothers (43:16–17). The brothers are nervous about being taken to Joseph's house. They feel that God is working against them to bring endless troubles into their lives. **It is the way we all feel when we are troubled with guilt**. Everything that happens we feel is a judgement upon us. We get nervous and anxious in God's world, feeling that everything is against us. *'This man is against us,'* they say (43:18). How wrong they are! All the time Joseph is arranging for their blessing, their provision, and their restoration to fellowship with himself. But the way he does it is to bring them to regret what they did. How can he possibly have friendship and fellowship with his brothers if they are plagued by guilt and shame over what they have done. Joseph has no choice. He must get them to break away from their past wickedness before he will be able to have fellowship and friendship with them.

It is the same with God. We often feel bad and nervous in His world and yet all the time the activities of God are not against us; they are designed to bring us to Himself. He has

98

to work in such a way that we admit our needs and our guilt There can be no deep fellowship otherwise.

They try to explain about the money (43:19–22) but Joseph puts them at their ease (43:23). He is nice to them. He brings Simeon out and cares for their needs (43:24). They hear that they are to have a meal with Joseph (43:25).

Then the meal begins. They give him the gifts they have for him (43:26; see 43:11), and he asks them about Jacob (43:27–28) and treats Benjamin his full brother with special affection (43:29). This is the way Jesus is toward us when He wants to bless us. Jesus does not reveal Himself when we are full of guilt as much as He does when we are at liberty and full of faith. He is not ready to reveal Himself to us while we believe that we are condemned. But while Jesus holds back from manifesting Himself to us, He is full of love. He cares about the details of our lives (*'He enquired about their welfare,'* 43:27).

Joseph is still not quite ready to reveal who he is but is overcome with loving affection for his family. He has to go out and weep because he cannot control himself (43:30). These brothers have sinned terribly against Joseph but Joseph has put all of that aside. He is holding nothing against them. He is so full of affection for them that it is almost overwhelming him. The love of Jesus is like this. We tend to think that He is against us – but that is nothing but guilt and the reflection of the way in which we would be in our dealings with others. Because we get vindictive when others sin against us we tend to feel that God gets vindictive when we have sinned against Him. But Jesus is not like that! Although these brothers have treated him so badly in the distant past, Joseph has nothing in his heart except concern for them and a desire to be fully restored to his old family.

Joseph comes back and the meal begins (43:31–32). They are amazed to find that the seating arrangements show detailed knowledge of the family (43:33). Jesus is like Joseph. Even at times when we are alienated from Him, the alienation is on our side not on His side. We have sinned against Him; He has not dealt badly with us.

Benjamin gets special treatment (43:34). The special treatment arose because Benjamin was Joseph's full brother. The others were half-brothers. Joseph loved them all but Benjamin his full brother, son of Rachel, was special. This is the way Jesus treats us. He is our brother. He is **the** Son of God, but we are adopted sons of God. Not biologically but spiritually we are Jesus' full brothers. We share His human nature; He shares our human nature. We come from the same human family. We have the same Father – God. Jesus treats us as His younger brothers. He is in wealth and glory and power but He is determined to *'bring many sons to glory'* (Hebrews 2:10). He plans to bring His brothers to be where He is in glory and wealth, ruling a mighty heavenly kingdom as Joseph was ruling Egypt. He wants to share all His wealth and knowledge and abundance with us.

1. It all shows that his previous rough treatment of them was for their good, not for his revenge. Joseph is far from showing any vindictive spirit.

2. It all shows a great deal of patience. Joseph must have been longing to reveal himself to them but they were not yet ready.

3. It shows great faith. Joseph is expecting that he will be able to bring them to the experience of God's forgiveness and to a good conscience before God.

Chapter 30

Joseph the Skilful Pastor

(Genesis 44:1–34)

Joseph releases his brothers, at the same time giving instructions that their money should be returned to them (44:1). Joseph's silver cup is to be put in Benjamin's sack (44:2). They leave in the morning (44:3) and soon Joseph's men catch up with them and demand to know why their have stolen Joseph's property (44:3–5). The brothers protest their innocence (44:6–8). *'With whomever of your servants it be found, let him die...'* (44:9). The cup is soon found in Benjamin's sack (44:10–12).

What is the point of Joseph's trick? He is not simply playing with them or being vindictive. **Joseph is testing the reality of his brothers' repentance**. It is his way of testing them to see what the relationships are between them and how they feel toward Jacob? Will they still betray one of the brothers for their own advantage? Will they still be totally unconcerned about the feelings of Jacob? The events that Joseph had brought about tested whether the brothers would still do the kind of thing they had done to him over twenty years before. Twenty years previously they had planned the death of Joseph. Now the death of Benjamin had been made easy for them by Joseph! How would they respond? Would they simply abandon Benjamin to his fate? Would they disregard Jacob's feelings and take revenge on his new favourite, Rachel's son Benjamin? Joseph wanted to know.

Joseph must have very eager to see what would happen. Would the brothers allow Benjamin to be brought back to Joseph for execution? It was wonderful for Joseph to see that a change had taken place in his brothers. They would not do again what they had done to Joseph many years previously. Years before they had taken trouble to get rid of Jacob's favourite Joseph; now they are taking trouble to do what they can to rescue Jacob's favourite, Benjamin.

The brothers make clear their very deep and real repentance. After Joseph's protest (44:14–15) Judah acts as a spokesman. *'God has exposed the guilt of your servants'* (44:16); he thinks Benjamin did indeed take the cup. He will not abandon Benjamin to his fate. He says they will all submit to being slaves in Egypt. He feels that what they did to Joseph has now come upon them. They are going to be slaves in Egypt just as they sold Joseph to slavery in Egypt years before. The brothers are admitting their guilt because they think they are being justly punished for what they did to Joseph. His fate is coming upon them

Then Joseph puts a special test before them. He offers them freedom on the understanding that Benjamin will remain as a slave (44:17). It is an exact replica of what they did to Joseph himself many years before when they sent Joseph off to be a slave but maintain freedom for themselves. How will they react now?

At this point Judah gives a very moving speech (44:18–34). **His speech reveals his great love for Jacob**. Years before they had cared nothing for Jacob when they got rid of Joseph, but now things have changed. Judah explains. Jacob loves Benjamin very greatly (44:18–20) and released him only very reluctantly (44:21–29). Jacob's life is bound up with Benjamin's life (44:30). If Judah goes back without Benjamin the grief for Jacob will be overwhelming (44:30–31). Judah is pleading for Benjamin out of his great love for his father Jacob.

His speech includes an offer to be a substitute for Benjamin. He has promised to be a surety for Benjamin and to bring him back safely (44:32). Now comes the most moving part of the speech. *'Let your servant . . . remain instead of the lad as a slave . . . '* (44:33). Out of great love for his father he wishes to substitute himself and release Benjamin. It is, of course, the precise thing that Jesus did on the cross. On the cross it was if as Jesus was saying to the Father 'Let Your servant remain instead . . . . ' 'Let Me be in the place of sinners.' 'Let Me bear your anger against sin instead of them.' Jesus offered Himself as our substitute. Judah is being Christ-like. 'Let me be Benjamin's substitute.' It demonstrates once and for ever that the brothers have changed and are deeply repentant over what they have done. Even when an opportunity is given them to have their own freedom but get rid of Benjamin, they will not take it. They would rather bear Benjamin's punishment in order that he will be restored to his father. Jesus was like that. He would rather bear our punishment so that we might be restored to the Father.

His speech reveals that Judah himself is a new man. Now we can understand why the story of Genesis 38 was put where it was between Genesis 37 and Genesis 39. It was the deep disgrace of the events recorded in Genesis 38 that was to humble Judah and lead into his being a man of humility and very great compassion. A sinner disgraced became a sinner restored with a very tender heart.

Joseph has now at last proved to his own satisfaction that these brothers have truly repented of the sin they had committed many years ago. If they were given a chance they now would not do what they had done years ago. When an opportunity to repeat the sin comes along they fight against it and stand by their brother Benjamin.

Joseph has had to do what he has done. What would be the good of bringing his family to Egypt if the old animosities and jealousies and hatred were still there? What would be the good of his having his brothers near him if they would kill him at the first opportunity?

But there is more. Not only has Joseph proved to his own satisfaction that the brothers have changed, **he has also allowed them to see that they have changed**. They have been put in the same situation that they were in years before and without knowing that they were dealing with Joseph they turned down all invitations to behave as they had done twenty years ago. They will have the joy of knowing that they have changed. They will have the joy of seeing that when they are placed in tempting situations they reject violently the temptations to repeat their old sin.

There is more still. **Joseph has provided enough evidence for Jacob to know that his sons have truly repented**. It is likely that Jacob will soon hear the entire story of what they did to Joseph. The terrible truth about the attempted murder and the abandonment in the pit and the sale to the passing Ishmaelites – it is all going to come out. Maybe Jacob will want to know every detail. What will he think of his sons? But Jacob has already provided evidence ahead of the event that the brothers have turned aside from such wickedness. The news of their sin and the news of their repentance will reach Jacob at the same time.

Joseph has been a skilful pastor and shepherd of his own family. He has brought them to repentance and he has made it possible for them and everyone involved to see that a very great change has taken place in their lives. They are ready to be a united family again – in Egypt.

Chapter 31

Protecting Forgiveness
(Genesis 45:1–28)

Joseph is now satisfied that the time has come for him to reveal himself. He is sure that the brothers are truly repentant over what they did many years ago.

1. **Joseph's forgiving spirit is so great he does not want anyone to know of their sin**. The story of what they had done is likely to come out if anyone is there at the time when Joseph reveals himself. So he sends the Egyptians away (45:1). His emotion is great (45:2). A godly man is likely to be warm-hearted and tender. When we forgive we do not even want anyone to know about how we have been hurt or injured.

2. **The brothers at first are terrified of Joseph**. They are speechless with fear (45:3). We can understand why. What awful crimes they had committed against Joseph! Now he is the most powerful person they know and they are at his mercy. When we feel the guilt of sinning – it is terrible.

3. **Joseph wants them to feel forgiven**. He has no wish to terrify them. *'Come close to me,'* he says. And then he reassures them. *'Do not be distressed and do not be angry with yourselves.'* God is like this. He does not want us to be heavily laden with guilt. The brothers have repented deeply. Joseph does not want them still to be burdened with guilt. God wants us to feel forgiven and Joseph is like God in this desire for his brothers to feel the burden of guilt lifted (45:4–5a).

4. **Joseph can see a purpose even in their sin** (45:5b–8a). God does not create sin, but He does control it and He does guide the way sin shows itself. God had steered the very

jealousy of Joseph's brothers so that it achieved His will. It is easier to forgive if you can see a purpose behind what has happened. Joseph wants to make it easy for them to forgive themselves. God was behind what had happened. *'God sent me ... God sent me ... It was not you who sent me here but God...'* (45:5, 7, 8). Joseph says it three times. He wants them to forgive themselves.

God uses human sin. The cross of Jesus was a wicked act but God was controlling sinners so that they achieved His will not their will.

5. **He wants them to feel reconciled to him**. He is an important person (45:8b). They must take the news back to Jacob and bring him to Egypt (45:9–13). He wants them to feel that he has nothing in his heart except loving concern for them. Despite the twenty years of suffering that they have caused him, Joseph wants them to feel so reconciled to him that it is as if it had never happened.

Many who 'forgive' others say 'I forgive you' but secretly hope the other person will feel burdened by what they have done. Joseph is not like that. He throws his arms round them. He weeps over them. He kisses them. Finally he convinces them that they truly are forgiven and that he has nothing against them at all. Then and only then do they feel free to talk with him (45:14–15).

6. **The family reunion has an affect on others**. The Egyptians get to hear about this loving family reunion (45:16). They know nothing about the betrayal and hatred of previous years. That has all been covered. Love covers a multitude of sins. But the loving harmony of Joseph and his brothers attracts the favour of Pharaoh who is extremely generous to Jacob and the whole family (45:17–20). Joseph sends gifts for them to take to Canaan to Jacob (45:21–24). Where there is loving unity among the people of God it attracts a lot of interest from others. People are looking for love and if they find it among the people of God they are interested and warm toward us.

7. **Joseph wants to protect the loving harmony of his family**. As they go he warns them: 'Don't quarrel on the way.' He

knows how feelings of guilt create quarrels. On the way back they are likely to be reviewing the past and this is likely to lead to blaming each other. They will start remembering whose idea it was to kill Joseph and then they will start remembering things that each one has done to the other or to Benjamin.

It is a major task of any kind of leader to protect the harmony and peace of his people. Joseph gives this word to them as they go because he knows he has to protect love. Love needs protecting. It requires thought and attention. It does not look after itself or take care of itself. Particular words of warning have to be given to protect love and peacefulness among the people of God.

8. **There is good news for Jacob**. Jacob could never have imagined that he would ever see Joseph again, but he will! They go back and tell him the good news (45:25–26) and he is amazed. It gives him new life (45:27) and he resolves to set out to see Joseph (45:28). The amazing grace and forgiveness of God spreads out further afield and influences one person after another. Something that Jacob wanted more than anything else in the world now is actually going to happen. He had loved Rachel passionately from the day he first set eyes on her. Then he had been devotedly attached to his and Rachel's two sons. He had lost Joseph for over twenty years but now he was about to see him again. The grace of God revives our hopes and brings about our greatest ambitions. Jacob wanted the kingdom of God to go forward and he wanted it to go forward through Rachel's oldest son. Now God was giving him the desire of his heart.

Chapter 32

A New Venture for Jacob

(Genesis 46:1–47:12)

'Israel' (as Jacob is sometimes called) is now to travel to Egypt. **Sometimes God calls us to new ventures at a time of life when we think we are going to be settled for the rest of our life**. Jacob never imagined that at that late stage in his life when he had been settled for many years in the land of promise, he would suddenly be called to spend the rest of his life in Egypt! He has never been to Egypt.

He gets confirmation of God's will before he travels. To leave Canaan to go to Egypt is a serious business. When Abraham did that it brought trouble (see Genesis 12:10–20). Isaac had once been forbidden to go there (see 26:2). It will involve a very different kind of life for him and he will never see Canaan again.

But as he worships God at Beersheba (46:1) God appears to him for the fourth time in his life (46:2) and confirms that he should go to Egypt. He need have no fear (46:3). The previous promises given to Isaac and to Abraham will be carried forward. 'Israel' and his descendants will become a nation while they are in Egypt. 'Israel' will be with Joseph for the rest of his life and he will come back as the nation of Israel in later years (46:4).

The predictions and plans of God get fulfilled. Many years before God had told Abraham that his descendants would be strangers in a land that was not theirs (see Genesis 15:13–14). God said that they would stay there in a foreign land for four hundred years and then the oppressive nation in which they stayed would be judged by God and God's people would be released.

Now the time has come. Jacob is in the purpose of God and is about to be used by God to bring about something which God had predicted many years before. Encouraged by God, Jacob with all his people and all his possessions leaves Canaan with the assurance that one day they will be back (46:5–7). The text of Genesis emphasizes that the entire people of Israel are there. There are thirty-three families mentioned in Genesis 46:8–14, including the six sons of Jacob via Leah (with Judah traced to a further generation). Another sixteen descended from Zilpah are mentioned in Genesis 46:15–18, including a woman Serah. The sons of Berah are traced to an extra generation.

There are fourteen families descending from Rachel's two sons (46:19–22) and another seven families descending from Bilhah (46:23–25). Leaving out two who had already died (46:12) and two who were born in Egypt sixty-six persons went to Egypt with their wives and children (46:26). If the two families of Er and Onan (46:12) are included plus the families of Joseph and Benjamin there were seventy (46:27).

Jacob is given the desire of his heart. A wonderful meeting takes place. Judah, who is now being regarded as the oldest son, goes to meet Jacob and the family arrives in Goshen (46:28). Then Joseph goes out to meet his father (46:29). What a day it was! They had not seen each other for more than twenty years. Jacob had never expected to see Joseph again. Joseph had longed for God's promises to him many years before to be fulfilled. When we commit our ways to God His promises will be fulfilled and He will give us the desires of our hearts. Jacob had loved Rachel with a passionate love ever since he had first seen her. Joseph was the oldest of her sons. All his life he had wanted Joseph to be someone special. Years before when Joseph predicted that he would be an eminent person admired by his family, Jacob had kept the saying in mind (see 37:11). Now the longings of his heart were fulfilled. Every desire which is within God's will will be given to us if we inherit it with faith and patience. Jacob's desires were given to him at last. He was a satisfied man, now that he had seen the face of Joseph (46:30). He was given a place of security, a place to call home for the rest of his life (46:31–47:6).

Jacob is given a continuing ministry. Jacob becomes a friend to Pharaoh, the most powerful man in the world in those days (47:7–10). He could never have dreamed that the day would come when he would be treated by Pharaoh with such respect and honour. It was a time of reward for Jacob. God likes to reward us. Of course Jacob's life had been full of ups and downs. There had been times of deceitfulness and immaturity. There had been times of self-pity when he swore he would spend the rest of his life in mourning. But now all the desires of his heart were given him. All his sufferings and trials were being counteracted. Despite the great sufferings Jacob had been through *'he will not often consider the years of his life, because God keeps him occupied with the gladness of his heart'* (Ecclesiastes 5:20). God is able to make it up to us for what we have suffered. Everyone who has left houses (as Joseph had left his house in Canaan) ... everyone who has lost brothers ... or children (as Joseph had left his brothers for many years and as Jacob had lost Joseph) ... shall receive many times as much (see Matthew 19:29). Jacob and Joseph received 'many times' what they had given to God and had the high privilege of being instruments in the forward move of God's kingdom.

Chapter 33

Skilful Leadership
(Genesis 47:13–31)

Now we discover how Joseph rose to very great power indeed. God had given him years of training both in his own character and in his ministry as a wise administrator. Now his skill shows itself as he becomes the administrator of the whole land of Egypt.

1. **Joseph refused to take glory for himself**. He was an ideal servant for Pharaoh because he brought very great profit and glory to Pharaoh and took none of it for himself. Many of God's servants want to take glory to themselves. Joseph had been like that in his teenage years. But now he had lost that self-glorifying spirit. He did what he did for Pharaoh.

Because of the neediness of the people (47:13) Joseph rose to absolute power. He required that the grain which he had stored should be bought, rather than be given away. First the people gave money (47:14); then they paid in livestock (47:15–17). Soon the livestock of the entire land belonged to Pharaoh. Then the people had no choice but to offer their lands and their freedom to Pharaoh (47:18–19). Joseph gave food in return for land (47:20) and the people of Egypt went wherever Joseph sent them (47:21). His wife's family were exempt (47:22); Joseph was married to a priest's daughter. A position of such great power was dangerous. Few men can rule an entire nation with such power in the way that Joseph did without that power becoming corrupting. But Joseph used the power that he had for the service of another. He got a lot of honour but he was happy to remain second to

Pharaoh. He did what he did for Pharaoh and was happy to live this way.

We should relate in this way to Jesus. The 'glory' we get for anything we do must not be stolen and taken for ourselves. Anything we do for God is not for ourselves. It is for Jesus. We are to be happy to have His name glorified.

Jesus Himself lived this way. He was content to do the will of the Father who sent Him. He said again and again that He was simply doing what God had sent Him to do. He was content that the honour should go to the Father. When God highly exalted Him and gave Him a name that is above every name, it was *'to the glory of God the Father.'*

God rewards us with honour. But it is what I call 'second grade honour'. The supreme honour goes to the Father; we live in the overflow of the honour that comes to Him. Our honour is to share His honour.

2. **Joseph became a model of power used wisely and generously**. Very great power came to him. Yet he used what power came to him in a way that ministered to the critical need of the people. He provided the seed for them to plant. He insisted that the seed should be used rather than stored or sold (47:23). A large amount of the produce should come back to Pharaoh again. He insisted that their profit should itself be used responsibly (47:24).

The people were content with this kind of slavery! It had saved their lives and they were immensely grateful (47:25). The period in which Joseph reigned led to the advantage of Pharaoh in a custom which lasted for a long time (47:26).

Almost any 'system of government' will work for the good of the people if it is used wisely and generously. The kind of slavery-to-Pharaoh that was being practised can hardly be regarded as a model system of government, and yet Joseph made it work for the good of the people. People often want to change 'systems of government' – both in the church and in the various governments of the world. But even a bad system can be used for good if the right person is in power. On the other hand a 'system' of government might be almost perfect but if there is selfishness and manipulation the

112

'system' will do little good. The characters of people are more important than systems and structures of management.

3. **Joseph's work led the people of Israel into a period of prosperity**. God's people flourished for a lengthy time in Goshen. Good leadership brings blessing for people – in the church and in the state. It is tragic when people are without a shepherd and wonderful when God gives good leadership. People need leaders. Most people lack drive and lack direction. Egypt would have been in a terrible plight if there had not been a man like Joseph to help them and guide them. His years of experience in Potiphar's house and in Pharaoh's dungeon had given him experience in organising people and organising programmes. As they were living under the leadership of Joseph, the people grew in number as God had predicted that they would (47:27; see 15:13–14). Joseph is just like Jesus. Jesus had supreme humility and lived in utter dependence on the Father. He has all authority and power and yet uses that authority to be head over all things for His people. Best of all, we flourish because we are under Him and submit to Him. In the case of earthly submission to an earthly ruler there are limits to our submission. We obey God rather than men. But our submission to Jesus knows no limits. Yet it is not painful submission but happy submission. Slavery to Him is freedom.

Chapter 34

Sovereign Graciousness
(Genesis 47:28–48:22)

Jacob expressed his faith that the purpose of God would continue after his death. He lived to a great old age (47:28) and when he knew he would die he expressed his certainty that God's promises would be fulfilled. He was confident that his descendants would go back to Canaan and he wanted to express publicly his faith that the future of God's people lay in Canaan. He wanted to be buried in Canaan as an expression of the fact that he was sure that it was there that God would work to bring blessing to the entire world (47:29–31a). *'Israel'* bowed in worship *'at the head of his bed'* or *'on his staff'* (47:31b).[1]

Few Christians give much thought to the impact they will have after they have gone home to heaven. Yet men and women of faith should be like Abel who *'still speaks, even though he is dead'* (Hebrews 11:4). Jacob's demand to be buried in Canaan would speak to later generations of the fact that he was living in expectation that God's future was in despised Canaan, not in luxurious and powerful Egypt. We too should give thought to ways of affecting later generations.

It is also to be noticed that Jacob was determined to serve God even in extreme old age. If God allows us to live to be very elderly we shall find that there are ways of serving Him even when we are frail and worn.

Jacob took steps to see that the promises of God were inherited by his children and grandchildren. After the oath which Joseph took (47:28–31) Jacob became ill and Joseph

114

went to see him with his two sons (48:1). Jacob wished to pass on the family promises. When Jacob dies the responsibility of carrying on the promises of God will rest with Joseph and his brothers. Jacob reviews the promises. God had promised the family of Abraham that his seed would be numerous and would inherit the land of Canaan (48:2–4). That promise had been passed to Isaac and to Jacob. Now Jacob wishes to pass it on to his twelve sons. He also wishes to specially honour the memory of Rachel his much-loved wife. Joseph was her son and Ephraim and Manasseh were her grandsons although she never saw them. Jacob makes a special arrangement. He adopts his two grandsons (Ephraim and Manasseh) as his own sons (48:5–6). Verse 7 gives his reason. He is thinking of Rachel and wants to honour her memory. The boys are identified (48:8–10); Joseph will not deceive him as Jacob himself had once deceived Isaac! He is so grateful to God for being allowed to see his grandchildren (48:11). Joseph formally hands his children over to Jacob (48:12); he is passing the inheritance to them.

Jacob blesses the boys in a way that underlines the fact that God often chooses the unexpected person to be the heir of His blessing. It would be normal for the firstborn son to get the greater blessing, but for two generations God has revealed His will that He wishes to choose the unexpected person. God had chosen Isaac not Abraham's much-loved Ishmael. God had chosen Jacob over the firstborn Esau. Jacob has learned a lesson. He knows that God might well give a special blessing to the unexpected person. It is this point that Jacob is expressing when, led by God, he deliberately gives a special blessing to Ephraim, crossing his hand to do so (48:13–14). Then he prays for Joseph, praying especially for the two boys (48:15–16a). He prays that they will have the faith to identify themselves with Abraham, Isaac and Jacob and the promise that has been passed down through them (48:16b).

Joseph does not like Jacob's treating the second-born as the firstborn and tries to get him to give the greater blessing to Manasseh (48:17–18) but Jacob is deliberately making the point that the firstborn according to human nature might not be the firstborn in God's choice (48:19–20). Both will have territory but the greater blessing will be for Ephraim.

The whole chapter is therefore about the right of God – and of Jacob! – to choose whoever He wants. God is sovereign and uses people in just the way He wants to. But His sovereignty is used in the interests of grace! When He chose Joseph, He *'meant it for good'* (see 50:20). When He chose the younger above the older, the younger had blessings also but He had purposes of grace in the way He would use the younger. Joseph chose Ephraim but he prayed for a blessing on both the two boys. This is the way God's sovereignty works. He chooses to use one and not another. He may even choose to save some and not others, but His long-term purposes are purposes of graciousness.

Jacob himself is underlining this point. His cross-handed blessing has given a little warning that God is a God of surprises. Now he makes the same point in another way. No one ever experienced the amazing sovereignty of God more than Jacob. *'Jacob have I loved!'* Jacob gives Joseph one mountain slope more than his brothers in the land of Canaan (48:21–22)! Genesis 48:22 refers to some previous conquering of Shechem about which we know nothing. I am sure Jacob was enjoying himself on his death bed! One last time before he died Jacob is still the same old Jacob. He gives preferential treatment to Joseph again, as he did years before with the coat with long sleeves! But again, it is a word of warning. God can give an extra blessing to whoever He likes! And so can Jacob! He did it before out of favouritism. This time he does it with deliberate purpose. It is a way of saying that God is the God of sovereign graciousness, a God whose freedom is such that no one can control Him or criticize Him. This time, the brothers will have to accept it without jealousy. They will have to accept sovereign graciousness.

Note

1. 'On his staff' is a possible translation if the Hebrew is read as *matteh* rather than *mittah*; the original Hebrew had no vowels. Hebrews 11:21 takes it this way. The other translation would be 'at the head of his bed'.

Chapter 35

Jacob's Farewell Prophecy
(Genesis 49:1–33)

Jacob is aware that he will soon die, and he is about to give his farewell prophecy. He calls his twelve children together (49:1–2) and has a word of assessment and prediction about each of them.

1. **There are three sons who have ruined their lives**. **Reuben** (49:3–4) was Jacob's firstborn son. As the firstborn son he should have been the ruler of the family but his instability and the sin mentioned in Genesis 35:22 caused him to be disinherited.

Simeon and **Levi** (49:5–7) had likewise ruined their lives by their display of violence and savagery in the incident of Genesis 34:25–26.

2. **There is one son with a glorious destiny**. The leadership of the family is given to **Judah**. We recall the story of his incestuous relationship with his daughter-in-law, in Genesis 38. Judah disgraced himself and revealed himself as a man of crudeness and brutality. When his daughter-in-law was found to be pregnant his only response was *'Bring her out and have her burned to death!'* (38:25). But then it was discovered that he was the father of her child.

This disgrace obviously had a powerful effect in Judah's life. The next time we meet him (in Genesis 43:8–9) he has become a compassionate man. His speech in Genesis 44:18–34 shows us how tender and merciful he became. His deep repentance led to his becoming a respected person within Jacob's family. The first three brothers, Reuben, Simeon and Levi all forfeited the right to be the leader of the family.

117

Judah had also sinned but his repentance was deep, and it was he that was given the privilege of being the leader and ruler of the family.

> ⁸ *Judah, your brothers shall praise you*
> *your hand shall be on the neck of your enemies*
> *your father's sons shall bow down before you.*
> ⁹ *Judah is a lion's whelp;*
> *you have grown up, my son, on prey.*
> *He crouches down, he reclined for sleep like a lion,*
> *like the king of the animals! Who dares to rouse him?*

Judah will be a royal tribe, honoured by all, the 'lion' among the tribes of Israel. However his role as the leader would be rewarded in a greater way than he ever could have imagined.

> ¹⁰ *The sceptre shall not depart from Judah,*
> *nor the ruler's staff from between his feet,*
> *until Shiloh comes,*
> *and the obedience of the nations comes to him.*

Judah will retain its sovereignty as the royal tribe until one particular person comes who is called 'Shiloh'. The phrase is difficult. It clearly refers to a person. It could be a phrase meaning 'He whose right it is'. Or – as I prefer to think – it could be a name. The Hebrew root *sh-l-h* is connected with peace. It could well mean 'the Peaceful One', in which case the royal tribe continues its dominion until 'the Peaceful One' comes. The word is feminine in form but takes a masculine verb. A name with a feminine-type structure could well function in this way. There is a town of the same name. 'Shiloh' (city of peace) was the place where the tabernacle was kept for many years. Later the tabernacle was kept at Jerusalem (a word which also means 'city of peace'!) It is not unknown for a word to be both the name of a person and of a place. 'Canaan' was a person before it was a place-name.

Whatever the precise meaning, 'Shiloh' will be a person of great rule: *'the obedience of the nations comes to him.'* Shiloh' will be a person of great wealth. He lets an ass eat valuable grapes. He washes his clothes in wine! (49:11). The days of 'thorns and thistles' will end and a land of abundant luxuriant vines and abundant wine will come instead! He has so much wine his eyes are red, and so much milk his teeth turn white (49:12).

There came a time in the history of the world when it looked as if the tribe of Judah had lost sovereignty, and it looked as if the house of David was totally useless. Suddenly in the tribe of Judah and in the house of David, came Someone who proved that Judah had not lost its kingship, and David's line was alive and well. Jesus was born in the line of David.

Shortly after Jesus' coming the tribe of Judah lost its identity. Jerusalem was destroyed in AD 70. The tribal records were lost and today no Jew knows what tribe he is from, and no one knows who descends from the line of David. The sceptre did not depart from Judah, until after Jesus had come – but then it was totally lost.

3. **There are eight sons whose future will be undistinguished**, **Zebulun** was given territory by the sea (49:13). The tribe of **Issachar** was given a very pleasant land and became a farming people (49:14–15). **Dan** was a small tribe but its strength was greater than its size (49:16–17).

Verse 18 is an interruption in the poem. *'I wait for your salvation, O Yahweh.'* Amidst all the various events that will come upon the tribes of Israel, salvation will come.

Gad had to constantly fight against invaders (49:19). **Asher** occupied fertile land and became prosperous (49:20). **Naphtali** will be productive (*'a productive deer, which brings forth beautiful fawns'*) and will live a peaceful nomadic life (49:21).

Joseph receives special attention. Despite his being like a fruitful and protective tree (49:22), he suffered much opposition in his early days (49:23). He remained strong (49:24) by the help of God (49:25). A number of names for God are strung together here to underline the greatness of God's protection: Jacob's Mighty One ... Shepherd ... Israel's Rock ... El Shaddai. An abundance of blessings came because of the way in which God used him (49:25b–26). Joseph is treated with warmth and favour but it is noticeable that nothing special is said about his future. The future of God's kingdom would be notable in the tribe of Judah, not in the Joseph-tribes of Ephraim and Manasseh.

Benjamin is the last to be mentioned. He is like a violent wolf (49:27). The poem ends (49:28) and after Jacob's request to be buried near the family of Abraham (49:29–32), we are told of his death (49:33).

None of these last eight tribes would produce anything as eminent as that which would happen through Judah. They would be seaside dwellers or farmers or fighters – but the kingdom of God would not go forward through the commonplace blessings of life. They would go forward through One chosen person, God's Elect, the Lion of the Tribe of Judah – our Lord Jesus Christ.

Chapter 36

God's Predestination
(Genesis 50:1–26)

Joseph had become a man of sensitivity. The suffering that
Joseph had endured had turned him into a man of love.
Suffering can push us in one of two directions: it can create
bitterness in us or it can soften us. Joseph was a man of
tenderness and loving graciousness to others. He was very
affectionate to his father and wept over him when his father
died (50:1).

Joseph had become a man of faith. He was expressing his
faith and his father's faith when he buried Jacob in Canaan
(50:2–7a). The promises of God did not concern Egypt; they
were about Canaan. Jacob had wanted to be buried in 'the
land of promise'. The family of Abraham had become
somewhat Egyptian in their ways. The people of Canaan
called them 'Egyptians' (50:11) but their sights were set on
God's promises in Canaan.

Joseph had become an honoured man. The Egyptians were
treating this family from Canaan with great honour. Many
Egyptian officials went with Joseph for a 'state funeral' in
Canaan (50:7b–11). Joseph had reached high honour in the
eyes of the Egyptians. God can do that for us when He wants
to. But it may not last. In the very next chapter of the Bible
there is *'a king who did not know about Joseph'* (Exodus 1:8).
We should not get too excited about honours from the
world. They do not last for ever. People might one day say
'Blessed is He who comes in the name of the Lord' but a little
later be saying *'Crucify Him!'* (Matthew 21:9; 27:23).
However a little bit of honour is nice while it lasts!

121

Joseph was a man who kept to his calling. God's promises were all connected with Canaan but Joseph was not tempted to stay there. He knew his calling concerned Egypt. He took one look at the 'land of promise' which he had not seen since he was seventeen years old, and then went back to the place where God had called him (50:1–14).

Joseph was gripped by his knowledge of the sovereignty of God (50:15–21). The doctrine of predestination is a mysterious subject but we have it here. It is a mystery. It cannot be explained. It is like the 'doctrine of the trinity' in being a total mystery and a stumbling-block to those who wish to expound Christian doctrine by means of human intelligence. It cannot be fathomed by human cleverness.

Joseph's brothers are afraid. They lose their assurance of Joseph's forgiveness (50:15) and this leads them in deceit (50:16–17) and into a spirit of bondage (20:18). But Joseph is living on the sovereignty of God. *'You meant it for evil . . . God meant it for good.'* He accepts the reality of human sin and the reality of human responsibility. 'You meant it . . . .' It was their sin. They had the spirit of hate and of jealousy. They planned Joseph's death and then decided to make money by selling him as a slave. They were responsible: 'you meant it'. But that is not the end of the story. 'God meant it' also. Joseph is happy to let the two statements stand side-by-side. 'You meant it . . . God meant it.' This is the mystery of what is sometimes called 'predestination and freewill'. God predestines; man is responsible. The two statements have to stay side-by-side (as also in Acts 2:23).

Joseph's conviction about the sovereignty of God helps him to forgive his brothers, and helps him to give assurance to them. He says to his brothers: 'It is alright. Don't worry. God was behind everything. God was using your mistakes to bring about something wonderful.' Joseph can forgive them because he believes that God was powerfully at work in what had happened.

Joseph's conviction about the sovereignty of God helps him to look back at the past (*'God intended it'*) and see God at work, and to look around at what is happening right now (*'to accomplish what is now being done'*) and gain strength. Joseph's conviction about the sovereignty of God helps him to give encouragement. *'Don't be afraid,'* he says, *'I will provide . . . .'* He reassured them and spoke kindly to them. It was his faith in the sovereignty of God that enabled him to speak this way.

Joseph was rewarded by a happy family life in his older years. He became a great-grand-father and enjoyed the warmth and company of his family (50:22–23). It was part of God's reward. For more than twenty years he had missed his family for the sake of what God was doing through him, but now what he had lost is made up to him.

Joseph was a man of faith until the end (50:24–26). The Christian life is a life of faith and more faith and faith again and again. Joseph had his eye on the purposes of God. In his last days he was giving encouragement to his family (*'God will surely come to your aid'*). He wanted his bones one day to be taken to Canaan.

Genesis ends at the point where Joseph has given instruction about his bones. Exodus tells us that Moses *'took the bones of Joseph with him'* (Exodus 13:19). The book of Joshua also ends by telling us that Joseph's bones were buried in Shechem (Joshua 24:32).

Joseph wanted to be remembered not as a famous Egyptian but as a believer in God's promises. He wanted to be known after his death as one whose sights were firmly fixed on the promises of God. Genesis ends by saying *'he was put in a coffin in Egypt'* (50:20) but Joseph had already made sure that his story would not end in a coffin in Egypt. When Hebrews speaks of the faith of Joseph it refers only to his dying words and his instructions about his bones (Hebrews 11:22). These bones were his way of saying that he was holding on to his faith in the promises unto the very end. Joseph believed in the promise of God and wanted everyone to know it.

More Advanced Reading

For preachers the following books may be recommended. I would think the four most useful works are the commentaries by Wenham, Hamilton, Leupold and Kidner. Gordon Wenham's two volumes (*Genesis 1–15*, *Genesis 16–50*, Word Biblical Commentary, Word, 1987 and 1994) are heavy and learned but contain much good material which the preacher should wrestle with if he is able to handle heavy scholarship. H.C. Leupold's *Exposition of Genesis* (2 volumes, Baker, 1963) is good but rather too literalistic in the early chapters, in my opinion. The best short volume is D. Kidner, *Genesis* (Tyndale, 1967). V.P. Hamilton's *The Book of Genesis* in two volumes (Eerdmans) is excellent. Allen P. Ross, *Creation and Blessing* (Baker, 1988) is an excellent exposition of Genesis.

The third edition and the fourth edition of the *New Bible Commentary* (Inter-Varsity, 1970 and 1994) are simpler and both have good commentaries on Genesis. One is by Meredith Kline; the other is a shorter version of Wenham's 2 volumes, compressed to 38 pages. *Matthew Henry's Commentary* (best read in its unabridged editions) is always good in narrative sections of the Old Testament.

Older works by C.F. Keil and F. Delitzsch (*The Pentateuch*, vol. 1, Eerdmans) and by Delitzsch alone *(New Commentary on Genesis*, 2 volumes, 1899) are heavy and technical but worth consulting. Westerman's volumes (*Genesis 1–11*, *Genesis 12–36*, *Genesis 37–50*) are often destructive; only those who wish to be well-informed need bother with them. Gispen's *Commentar Op Het Oude Testament, Genesis* (3 volumes, Kok, Kampen, Holland) is good

for Hebraists who read Dutch! Among weighty commentaries J. Calvin's *Genesis* (reprinted Banner of Truth, 1975) is
one of the best. R. Candlish's *An Exposition of Genesis*
(various editions; mine is by Sovereign Grace, 1972) is
old-fashioned but good. I seem no longer to have Basil
Atkinson's *Genesis* (published by Walter). I recall I liked his
odd little volume and found it packed with good exposition
as well as eccentricities. Something similar could be said of
A.W. Pink's exposition of Genesis. E.A. Speiser's *Genesis* is
of little value for preachers. Cassuto's volumes need not
trouble us. I love Martin Luther's eight volumes on *Genesis*;
they do not keep to the text in a disciplined way but are
always interesting and surprisingly helpful in obscure places.
I have never made much use of Philips, *Exploring Genesis*,
since alliteration is not my style, but I think some would find
his lay-out helpful in preaching.

Among works on parts of Genesis, E.J. Young's *Genesis
One* (Presbyterian and Reformed) is good and is found in
simplified version in *In the Beginning* (Banner of Truth). His
work on Genesis 3 is spoiled, in my opinion, by his thinking
that the story of 'the snake' is meant to be taken as a literal
story about an animal. Blocher's work on Genesis 1–3 is
excellent. Works by Joyce Baldwin (*The Message of Genesis
12–50*, IVP, 1986), R.S. Wallace (*Abraham*, Nelson, 1981)
and R.T. Kendall (*God Meant It For Good*, various editions;
All's Well That Ends Well, Paternoster, 1998) are valuable.

If you have enjoyed this book and would like to help us to send a copy of it and many other titles to needy pastors in the **Third World**, please write for further information or send your gift to:

Sovereign World Trust
PO Box 777, Tonbridge
Kent TN11 0ZS
United Kingdom

or to the **'Sovereign World'** distributor in your country.

Visit our website at **www.sovereign-world.org**
for a full range of Sovereign World books.